Trends in Marriage

ISSUES

Volume 106

Editor

Craig Donnellan

 *Independence*

Educational Publishers
Cambridge

First published by Independence
PO Box 295
Cambridge CB1 3XP
England

British Library Cataloguing in Publication Data
Trends in Marriage– (Issues Series)
I. Donnellan, Craig II. Series
306.8'1

ISBN 1 86168 326 X

Printed in Great Britain
MWL Print Group Ltd

Typeset by
Lisa Firth

Cover
The illustration on the front cover is by
Pumpkin House.

CONTENTS

Introduction

Trends in Marriage is the one hundred and sixth volume in the **Issues** series. The aim of this series is to offer up-to-date information about important issues in our world.

Trends in Marriage looks at marriage and cohabiation as well as separation and divorce.

The information comes from a wide variety of sources and includes:
Government reports and statistics
Newspaper reports and features
Magazine articles and surveys
Website material
Literature from lobby groups
and charitable organisations.

It is hoped that, as you read about the many aspects of the issues explored in this book, you will critically evaluate the information presented. It is important that you decide whether you are being presented with facts or opinions. Does the writer give a biased or an unbiased report? If an opinion is being expressed, do you agree with the writer?

Trends in Marriage offers a useful starting-point for those who need convenient access to information about the many issues involved. However, it is only a starting-point. At the back of the book is a list of organisations which you may want to contact for further information.

*****

The family then and now

Information from FamilyOnwards

Was there ever a golden time for the family? Perhaps in our mind's eye we like to hold onto a picture of the stability and strength of the Victorian family, a time when 'father knew best' and everyone was aware of their place. Well, just possibly this was an era when, for some, there was the security of a large family – where the unmarried aunts, for example, were taken in and lived with their married brethren. However, we also know that it was a time when the majority struggled against poverty, illness, and squalor. And countless people did not have the safety net of a family, and found themselves out in the cold because of an illegitimate child, or some other reason, and were unable to care for themselves in old age.

We do know that after World War Two there were great upheavals in family life when the troops came home. Children and fathers were trying to get to know each other after a long absence, or even seeing each other for the first time. In the UK children were returning home from being evacuated and mothers, who had coped alone during those years, had to learn to be part of a family or a couple again. Very many marriages did not survive, and the divorce rate escalated. I believe the disruption of those years had a great knock-on effect on future generations, when twenty or so years later the children of that period, who had been deprived of a settled home with two parents, went on to become parents themselves.

Perhaps we think of the fifties and sixties as a time when a mother, father, two children and a dog frolicked through life. But was that picture any more real? The divorce rates and the number of broken families were soaring, and although we knew that there were – and always have been – mothers and fathers on their own, 'single-parent family' was not yet part of our vocabulary.

What will people in years to come think about life in the early years of the twenty-first century? The media have been very willing to come up with evidence to show the 'death of the family', and to illustrate this by telling us about the abuse of the elderly, the trauma for children of broken marriages, and the rise in the number of teenage pregnancies. Every day we read of distraught fathers forbidden to see their children after a family breakup, and at the same time read, too, of fathers who will not pay child-support and who do not see the benefit of keeping in touch with their children. We are told that Britain has the highest rate of teenage pregnancies in Western Europe. We are shocked by the revelations of child prostitution, young people sleeping rough, and are urged to help put a full stop to child cruelty and abuse.

Yet if we consider the high viewing figures for nightly 'soaps' it suggests that there is a great interest in family life, even if it is only representative of dysfunctional television families. There is a fascination about the way relationships unfold on our screens. The irony is that the families eating fast food in front of the television, watching the family dramas unfold, often neglect their own households. Family life needs constant maintenance and care.

Families today have a variety of different labels, but whether 'traditional', 'step', 'blended', 'child-free', 'gay' or 'one-parent' what is important is the interaction between members of the family: how they look after each other and whether there are people to turn to, to huddle with, if the outside world is cold.

> *If we consider the high viewing figures for nightly 'soaps' it suggests that there is a great interest in family life*

Are you aware that the definition of a family in the UK today still includes more than one generation? Remember, too, that there are couples married for almost a lifetime and whose relationships do not make headline news. The chemistry of each family is different and each family must find its own way of creating strong links between its members, while also allowing each of them to preserve an individual identity.

The family may not be as recognisable as it once was, but it is still alive and thrives in a variety of ways. As well as the old, there are new patterns, and we must learn to make room for them and to value them.

Perhaps there never has been a golden age of the family: we can only try to do the best we can in bringing up our own children, watching out for other family members, caring for the sick and our elderly, and hope that by doing so we are laying the seeds for a caring, loving community in the future. Is that really too much to ask?

■ Information from FamilyOnwards – see page 41 for address details.

The family today

An at-a-glance guide

During the 20th century, improved health and living standards meant that people lived longer, more active lives along with more leisure time and the means to enjoy it. Families became smaller as the birth rate fell and women married, then had children, at a later age. More women remained childless. The number of households increased. More people lived alone and more single parents established their own household. More couples lived together, or divorced and remarried. The part that the family plays in our everyday lives is also changing. As we move into the 21st century, most people will spend a much smaller part of their active life bringing up dependent children. Only one-fifth of households are made up of a married couple with dependent children.

Family life

21st-century parents spend an average of about an hour and a half a day with their children – helping with homework, swimming, talking, sorting out problems or visiting museums and theme parks. This compares with an average of half an hour a day in the 1970s.

When families in the UK were asked to make their family trees, they discovered tens and hundreds of connections to cousins or step-relatives and their families – people whom they had not spoken to or kept in touch with for many years.

But when families in the USA were asked what makes a family, the majority answered that doing things together was most important.

So although the feeling of belonging to a family is the most important thing in life for approximately three in four people in the UK today, day-to-day contact with family is quite different.

Only one-fifth of households are made up of a married couple with dependent children

More people include close friends in the wider circle of family – often providing emotional support on a day-to-day basis.

There are more four and five generation families today than there were one hundred years ago.

Eleven per cent of changes in households including older people happen when younger generation adults move back into the family home.

At the beginning of the 21st century, around one in three families have a home computer.

More than 13 million people have access to the Internet and half the population has a mobile phone. New technology makes it easier for family members to keep in touch across distances.

Around 18 per cent of women aged 45 to 49 and 19 per cent of men aged 50 to 54 years care for aged parents.

In a survey sixty-one per cent of grandparents in Great Britain said they saw their grandchildren at least once a week in 2001.

Who is the family today?

There are just over 16 million families and 12 million children in the UK today.

Seventy-eight per cent of children lived in a household headed by a couple in 2002.

In 2000 there were 300,000 marriages in the United Kingdom; this was the first year that marriages had increased since 1992.

In 2000 there were 126,000 remarriages, accounting for two-fifths of all marriages.

There are an estimated 1.75 million one-parent families in Britain today – one-quarter of families.

In 2002, 4.5 million people (or eight per cent) in the United Kingdom described themselves as belonging to a minority group.

By the end of the 20th century just over 50,000 children were looked after in residential care.

There were just under 6000 adoptions in England and Wales in 2001.

Over a third of children in the UK were living in poverty in 1999 compared to only one in ten in 1979. Over half (62 per cent) of lone parents live in poverty. 30 per cent of children live in a family without a full-time worker.

In 2001, almost nine in ten people aged 60 and over in Great Britain were grandparents.

In 2002 the average size of Bangladeshi and Pakistani households was 4.7 and 4.2 people respectively. Average sizes of Black Caribbean, Mixed origin and White households were each around 2.3 people.

Over the last decade the average age of women at the birth of their first child had risen by 1.5 years to reach 27 years in 2000.

Marriage and relationships

Just over half the adult population of Great Britain are married.

Nine out of ten couples living with their children are married.

In Great Britain a quarter of non-married adults aged 16 to 59 were co-habiting in 2002.

In 2001, 14 per cent of adults aged 16 to 59 reported at least one cohabiting union that did not lead to marriage, with almost a quarter of people aged 30 to 34 reporting such a union.

There were 157,000 divorces granted in 2001, the first rise since 1996.

Although the divorce rate peaked in 1993, two in five marriages will still ultimately end in divorce.

Over a quarter of divorces in 1999 were granted to people married for between five and ten years.

Almost 60 per cent of divorces in 1999 were granted to couples where the woman was under 25 when they first married.

Fifty per cent of divorces were granted to couples with children in 1999.

In 1999 two-fifths of all marriages were of couples where at least one of the partners had been married before.

There were over 10,000 more divorces granted in the early 1990s than by the end of the 20th century.

1.3 per cent of couples are from different ethnic backgrounds.

In 2000 the average age at first marriage in England and Wales was 30 for men and 28 for women, compared to 25 and 23 respectively in 1961.

The median duration of marriage for couples divorcing in 2000 was 11 years.

The average age at which people got divorced in England and Wales in 2000 was 41 years for men and 38 years for women; compared to 39 years and 36 years respectively in 1971.

In 2000 almost 10 per cent of men and women were divorced.

A third of men and a quarter of women were single in 2000, compared to a quarter of men and a fifth of women in 1971.

The largest increase in the proportion of households containing people living alone has been among men aged under 65, more than tripling from three per cent of households in 1971 to 10 per cent by 2000. These increases reflect the decline in marriage, the increase in age at first marriage, and the rise in separation and divorce.

Lone parents

In spring 2002 around a fifth of dependent children in Great Britain lived in lone-parent families, almost twice the proportion in 1981.

Between 1971 and 1991 the proportion of lone-parent households with dependent children doubled, from three to six per cent. The proportion then remained at around this level up to 2002.

Almost one in five dependent children live in lone-mother families.

Lone-father families accounted for two per cent of all families with dependent children in 2000.

One-parent families are now a stage in the life cycle lasting about five years.

One in seven lone mothers has never married or lived with the father of their child.

Twelve per cent of lone parents were male in 2002.

The average age at which people got divorced in England and Wales in 2000 was 41 years for men and 38 years for women; compared to 39 years and 36 years respectively in 1971

The median age for a lone parent is 35. Lone fathers tend to be older, with the largest proportion being in their forties.

Three per cent of lone parents are teenagers.

Around 40 per cent of families with children headed by a black person or someone of mixed origin, were lone-parent families. This compares with a quarter of families headed by a white person and 10 per cent of families headed by an Asian person.

Stepfamilies

Eighty-eight per cent of stepfamilies consisted of a couple with one or more children from the previous relationship of the female partner.

In 2001 stepfamilies accounted for eight per cent of families with dependent children whose head was aged under 60 in Great Britain.

This article summarises the key facts about the family in the UK today in an 'at a glance' format. Most of the information comes from government sources and research reports commissioned by industry, charities or think tanks. These organisations commission studies that paint a picture of the family today in Britain so that they can plan policy and services as well as predict future trends. Sometimes researchers have to keep pace with changes that are happening very quickly. Sometimes trends are known to exist but there is no hard evidence. For example, there is little information about the numbers of children growing up in 'unofficial' stepfamilies (where neither partner is remarried or cohabiting full-time) or in part-time stepfamilies (where the child-ren spend time with both parents in turn), in gay families or in families where parents are each from a different religion or culture.

■ The above information is from a factsheet produced by the National Family and Parenting Institute (NFPI) – visit www.nfpi.org for references. For more inform-ation see page 41 for their address details.

© NFPI 2003

Changing marriage

Information from One Plus One

Changing views

Getting married is still popular in Britain, with most people marrying at some point in their lives. However, the social role and meaning of marriage has changed.

The traditional view of marriage, as the gateway to adulthood and independence, has become less prevalent over the last generation. A One Plus One study[1] of marriage in the early 1980s showed that the attractiveness of marriage lay partly in the fact that it provided a 'package of rights', guaranteeing immediate transition to adulthood. Today, it is more socially acceptable for couples to begin a sexual relationship, set up home, and have children outside formal marriage.

Evidence from the British Social Attitudes Survey[2] suggests that all age groups have changed their views. However, rather than attitudes changing markedly with age, people's views are largely shaped by the influences of the social climate within which they have grown up.

For example, there are dramatic differences between the views of those aged 55 and above and younger people. The most notable shifts in attitudes are among 35- to 54-year-olds.[2]

Traditional views are more likely to be held by religious and married people. Differences in educational background are also indicators of differences in attitudes: those without qualifications hold more traditional views than those with them. How-ever, those with higher educational qualifications are more traditional in their outlook than those with lower qualifications.[2]

Emerging patterns

Between 1984 and 2000, the pro-portion of people thinking there is 'nothing wrong' with pre-marital sex increased from 42% to 62%, while the proportion thinking it to be always wrong decreased from 17% to 9%.[2] It is increasingly uncommon for first sexual intercourse to take place within marriage. In 2000, around two-thirds of people saw cohabitation as perfectly acceptable – in fact, over half thought it was 'a good idea' for couples intending to get married.[2] More than 70% of first partnerships are now cohabitations.[3] 73% of people aged under 35 and living in cohabiting unions expect to marry each other – about one in eight never expect to marry.[4]

85% of people aged 65 or above think that marriage and parent-hood should go hand in hand, compared with just over a third of 18- to 24-year-olds. However, even among the most traditional groups, views about the relationship between marriage and parenthood have changed.[2]

In 1989, almost 75% of the population believed that 'people who want children ought to get married'. Five years later, in 1994, this had fallen to 57%; now, just over half the population subscribe to this view.[2] In 2003, just over 40% of births were outside mar-riage,[5] more than four times the proportion in 1975.

Attitudes to marriage and cohabitation [2]			
	Agree %	Disagree %	Neither %
Married couples make better parents than unmarried ones	27	43	28
Even though it might not work for some people, marriage is still the best kind of relationship	59	20	20
Many people who live together without getting married are just scared of commitment	36	34	28
Marriage gives couples more financial security than living together	48	28	22
There's no point in getting married - it's only a piece of paper	9	73	16
Too many people just drift into marriage without really thinking about it	69	10	19

Base: 2980.

Marriage as the ideal

One survey[6] shows that, when presented with a range of lifestyles to choose from, 68% of those questioned chose 'being married and with children' as their preferred lifestyle, and 77% disagreed with the statement that 'marriage is dead'.

Young people also reaffirm the symbolic significance of marriage. A survey[7] exploring young people's lives in Britain today found that only 4% agreed with the statement 'Marriage is old-fashioned and no longer relevant' and 89% said that they would like to get married at some time in the future.

However, findings from the British Social Attitudes Survey suggest that, whilst marriage is still widely valued as an ideal, it is regarded with much more ambivalence in terms of everyday partnering and parenting.

Analysis of marriage expectations suggests that cohabiting couples are less likely to marry their present partner once they have had a baby: a larger proportion of women with children than childless women (60% compared with 45%) never wish to marry their present partner, and the results are similar for men (66% compared with 47%).[4]

Ermisch (2000)[4] suggests that this may partly be explained by the uncertainty some couples have about making a commitment. Couples unsure about marrying each other are more likely to have a child in a cohabiting union, while cohabiting couples who plan to marry, marry first and then have children.

Further analysis of data on marriage expectations suggests that 15-20% of never-married, childless people aged between 16 and 35 do not expect to marry at all.[4]

Changing emphases
'Institutional' v 'Relational'

Romantic love is usually portrayed in our culture as the single most important motive for marriage. Nevertheless, research at One Plus One[1] has found that many factors inspire newlyweds to marry – a gradual feeling of disillusionment about being single, fears of growing old alone, and perceptions that they were now 'ready' for marriage – as much as the desire for matrimony.

Two models of marriage[12]	
Institution	**Relationship**
- Less freedom of choice of marriage partners	- Greater freedom of choice
- Marriage linked to wider societal and/or kinship obligations	- Marriage relatively separate from wider social and/or kinship obligations
- Emphasis upon economic aspects of marriage e.g. property and the sexual division of labour	- Emphasis upon the emotional and personal aspects of marriage
- Public emphasis	- Private emphasis
- Marriage as one of a set of social relationships	- Marriage as the central adult relationship
- Relative inequality within marriage; patriarchy	- Relative equality within marriage; companionship
- Little emphasis on mutual sexuality; sexuality linked to procreation	- Positive emphasis on sexuality; sexual dysfunction seen as sign of marital problems

Morgan (1992),[8] along with other commentators, sees the nature of marriage as moving from an institutional to a relational/companionate model. Burgess and Locke (1945)[9] describe how, in the past, the unity of family life was shaped in relation to the formal authority of the law, tradition, public opinion and ritual, and a rigid disciplinary system. By treating 'marriage' and 'the family' as social institutions, family practices are organised and understood in relation to particular external standards and values.

In contrast, the emergence of a new family form – the companionate family – saw interpersonal relations between spouses as the linchpin of family life. Stone (1979)[10] discusses how an early rise in relational/companionate marriage began in the 18th century (particularly among the upper and middle classes), when future spouses started to have more freedom to choose marriage partners for themselves.

Many of these young people put the prospect of emotional satisfaction before the ambition for increased income or status. This, in turn, helped to equalise relationships between husband and wife. Partners began to address each other in more affectionate terms and were more likely than before to set up home on their own, away from their families. A 'honeymoon' period during which the young couple were left to get to know each other sexually and emotionally became an accepted ritual.

Whilst the value attached to equality and sharing in modern marriage has certainly increased in the last 50 years, behaviour within marriage is still highly influenced by the institutional model of marriage. In particular, the reality of married life continues to be one of relative inequality around domestic duties.

Although women's participation in paid work has greatly increased during the 20th century, this has not been matched by an increase in men's participation in household and caring work. The relational changes between men and women can be seen in terms of 'lagged adaptation',[11] whereby men have been slower to respond to the changes in women's attitudes and practices.

It is important to bear in mind that the 'institutional' and 'relational' models of marriage are ideal types: modern marriages usually

contain elements of both. Economics, for example, play an important part in the processes and negotiations of married life, if not in the initial choice of partner.

Similarly, historians and family researchers express scepticism about whether the modern marital relationship is inspired entirely by private romantic ideals. Weddings, for instance, represent an important way for couples to add public recognition to their personal commitment.

Over the life cycle of a marriage, relational or institutional elements are likely to predominate at different times. In the early years, when romantic love is at a peak, the relational form may be more pronounced. After the arrival of children, marriages usually undergo changes which more accurately reflect institutional marriage. Domestic chores become increasingly segregated along gender lines, wider family such as grandparents become more involved in the young family's life, and the presence of children means that the State starts to take more interest in the private world of the couple.

After children leave home the marriage may move back to a more companionate form, with the couple devoting more time to each other – with increased longevity this period can last up to 30 years.

His or her marriage?

Married women talk about 'togetherness' in marriage and sharing a 'common life' with their husbands (by this they mean sharing interests and time with their partner). Men,

---

Between 1984 and 2000, the proportion of people thinking there is 'nothing wrong' with pre-marital sex increased from 42% to 62%

---

on the other hand, maintain a concept of togetherness that contains elements of traditional marriage. They are more likely to emphasise the importance of knowing that a wife can be a source of support if necessary, and are less likely to stress the need to have time for talking together. Young husbands' views of togetherness have more to do with geographical than emotional closeness (Mansfield and Collard, 1988).[1]

It is possible that the women's movement has been an important catalyst in the progress towards an increasingly strong emphasis on equality and sharing in marriage. Women seem to have moved towards the relationship model of marriage earlier and at greater speed than men.

REFERENCES

1. Mansfield P, Collard J (1988) *The beginning of the rest of your life?* (Basingstoke: Macmillan.)
2. Barlow A, Duncan S, James G, Park A (2001) Just a piece of paper? Marriage and cohabitation. In A Park, J Curtice, K Thomson, L Jarvis, C Bromley (2001/2002 edition) *British Social Attitudes: Public policy, social ties.* (London: SAGE Publications.)
3. Ermisch J, Francesconi M (2000) Patterns of household and family formation. In R Berthoud, J Gershuny (Eds) *Seven years in the lives of British families: Evidence on the dynamics of social change from the British Household Panel Survey.* (Bristol: The Policy Press.)
4. Ermisch JF (2000) *Personal Relationships and Marriage Expectations: Evidence from the 1998 British Household Panel Study* (Working Paper: Institute for Social and Economic Research, University of Essex.)
5. National Statistics (2004) Report: Live births in England and Wales, 2003: area of residence. *Population Trends*, no 116 (London: The Stationery Office.)
6. MORI Polls and Surveys (1999) *Family and Marriage Poll* (MORI Corporate Communications.)
7. The Opinion Research Business (2000) *Young People's Lives in Britain Today.* (London: The Opinion Research Business.)
8. Morgan D (1992) Marriage and society: understanding an era of change. In J Lewis, D Clark, D Morgan (Eds) *Whom God hath joined together.* (London: Routledge.)
9. Burgess EW, Locke HJ (1945) *The family: from institution to companionship.* (New York: American Book Publishers.)
10. Stone L (1979) *The family, sex and marriage in England 1500-1800.* (Harmondsworth: Penguin.)
11. Gershuny J, Godwin M, Jones S (1994) The Domestic labour revolution: a process of lagged adaptation. In M Anderson, F Bechhofer, J Gershuny (Eds) *The social and political economy of the household.* (Oxford: Oxford University Press.)
12. Reynolds J, Mansfield P (1999) The effect of changing attitudes to marriage on its stability. In *High divorce rates: The state of the evidence on reasons and remedies.* Vol 1. 1999. (London: The Lord Chancellor's Department Research Secretariat.)

■ This information is produced by One Plus One, the leading relationship research and training organisation. For more information see page 41 for their address details or visit www.oneplusone.org.uk.

Breaking uneven

Cohabitees who split up have none of the rights enjoyed by married couples after a divorce. But with the numbers of unmarried partners expected to soar, the government is about to take action

By Clare Dyer

Emily and Douglas lived together for 18 years until, five months ago, he moved out. 'He said he was having a breakdown and I thought he really was until I went to visit one evening and found two dressing gowns hanging on the back of the door and realised he'd got somebody else.'

That was just the first shock. Douglas, a self-employed businessman in his late 40s, earns at least £90,000 a year, and five years ago Emily gave up her job as a teacher to help him out by doing work he brought home from the office and helping to entertain clients. When he left, he initially agreed to give her £1,000 a month maintenance but then changed his mind and stopped the payments. Although her name is on the deeds of the flat they shared, where he is allowing her to stay for the moment, 'it's been mortgaged up to the hilt and there will be very little profit when it's sold', she says. She has found work as a supply teacher, earning between £200 and £500 a month, and is applying for full-time jobs but recognises that, at 54, her age counts against her.

The next shock came when she consulted a solicitor and found out just how little protection the law gives her. Had she been married to Douglas, she might have expected to receive enough to buy herself a home, and, possibly, maintenance for a time. 'My solicitor told me I was not entitled to anything except my share of the flat and the joint bank account, which is £5,000 in the red. I'm an intelligent woman but I didn't realise I don't have the same rights as a married woman.'

Her story harks back to the cautionary tale of Valerie Burns, who first took her case to court in 1980. She lived with Patrick Burns for 19 years, changed her name to his and looked after the home – bought in his name – and the couple's two children, who were 17 and 18 when their parents split up. For five years before she left him, in 1980, she worked and bought household equipment and furniture, though she didn't contribute to the mortgage.

Burns v Burns went all the way to the court of appeal but at the end Mrs Burns was left empty-handed. As Lord Justice May put it at the time: 'I think that she can justifiably say that fate has not been kind to her. In my opinion, however, the remedy for any inequity she may have sustained is a matter for parliament and not for this court.'

Families have changed dramatically in the past 25 years, with many more couples now choosing to forgo marriage, even after children arrive. Yet the legal consequences today are much the same as they were in 1980. Wives – and husbands – who divorce have a right to claim maintenance, a lump sum, and a share of any family property, even if it is in the other partner's name. Cohabitees who split up have no such rights. If the family home happens to be in their ex-partner's name, they face a complicated legal battle depending on principles of 19th-century trust law, which may not help in their particular case.

More than two decades later, parliament has still provided no remedy for today's equivalent of Valerie Burns. A woman who took part in a recent research study of cohabitation breakdown was shocked to discover she had no right to a share of the family home in which she'd lived for 18 years and brought up her children.

Cohabitees who split up. . . face a complicated legal battle depending on principles of 19th-century trust law

But with the numbers of cohabiting couples predicted to soar from two million today to 3.8 million over the next 25 years, the government is poised to take action. Stronger rights for cohabitees is not yet formal government policy in England and Wales, but the Lord Chancellor, Lord Falconer, has asked the law commission, the official law reform body, to draw up proposals. A consultation paper is planned for spring 2006, with final recommendations and a draft bill around July 2007.

North of the border, the Family Law (Scotland) Bill, introduced in the Scottish Parliament last month (February 2005), will allow cohabitees to make limited financial claims on the other partner when the relationship breaks down and will strengthen their position when the other partner dies without a will.

Pressure for change has been building up over the five years since Dame Elizabeth Butler-Sloss, England's senior family judge, predicted that the law would have to provide more protection for unmarried partners: 'The most likely thing is that parliament will be asked to provide something short of marriage by way of provision for those who are not married,' she told the Mothers' Union in 2000. 'There is a great discussion at the moment that men and women who cohabit are done down because they do not have the same rights as married couples.'

The Civil Partnerships Act 2004 will allow same-sex couples to register their unions from autumn 2005, giving them most of the rights married couples enjoy. The government resisted calls for the same rights to be extended to opposite-sex couples, arguing that they, unlike gay partners, had the option to marry.

But proponents of change say registration is not the answer because most cohabiting couples who have simply not got round to marrying would be equally unlikely to register their partnership. Surveys show that most are simply unaware of how few rights they have.

A recent survey for the government-funded Living Together Campaign, launched to inform cohabiting couples about their lack of rights, found that 61% thought they were in 'common law' marriages, which conferred the same rights as formal wedding vows. The reality is that common law marriage has not existed in England since 1753 (a form of common law marriage still exists in Scotland, but most cohabiting couples would not come within the strict rules).

The law commission will not propose equating cohabitation with marriage, but will suggest a package of remedies for those who suffer hardship when a relationship breaks down or a partner dies, according to Stuart Bridge, the law commissioner heading the project. The Law Society and the Solicitors' Family Law Association (now called Resolution) have come up with separate but similar blueprints on which the commission will be able to draw. The Law Society's proposals would give a cohabitee a right to apply for capital, such as a share of the family home, if the couple broke up after living together for two years or after having a child together. There would also be a limited right to apply for maintenance, but only in exceptional cases would this last longer than four years.

Death can bring a double blow for the survivor of a cohabiting couple. When her partner Stan died, 68-year-old Joan lost her financial security as well. The pair had worked together on the 60-acre west country farm he owned when he was suddenly taken ill. She consulted a solicitor about making wills but before it could happen Stan died. Much to her surprise, she discovered she had no right to inherit the farm. Without a will, it would go to Stan's adult children from his former marriage.

61% surveyed thought they were in 'common law' marriages, which conferred the same rights as formal wedding vows

---

Joan wanted to go on farming and claimed a share of the estate under the law which allows dependants to stake a claim after death. The result was a lengthy, expensive and acrimonious court battle with Stan's family. Joan wanted to buy a smallholding but instead she was awarded £70,000 and the right to live in a £280,000 house in a town, which would revert to the family when she died. She never lived there and the case was still rumbling on when she died. 'She really couldn't understand, having spent most of her life working her butt off on the farm, why the law shouldn't give her the farm,' recalls her solicitor, Ian Downing. 'She was never prepared to accept the law was as it was.

'It was a classic case of a couple who had no concept at all that there was no such thing as a common law marriage. I'm sure he never intended to leave her unprovided for.

'I've got very little doubt that it did shorten her life because I think ultimately she just lost interest in life. I got a very strong impression that she really felt life had cheated her out of everything she was expecting. Her view was "we never made pension provision, we were going to wind the farm down and we were going to live our old age with what we'd put together" and she saw all that taken away from her.'

■ The couples' names have been changed. For the Living Together Campaign visit their website at www.advicenow.org.uk

Origins of the myth of common-law marriage

Information from One Plus One

The myth of common-law marriage – that couples who live together have the same legal rights as married couples – springs from a time when there was uncertainty about what constituted a marriage. Church and State marriage ceremonies are relatively recent – grafted onto older popular rites whose legitimacy was not dependent on written law.

Marriage by consent

In earlier times, the validity of a marriage depended on the consent of the two parties publicly announced or at least symbolised by the exchange of rings or love tokens. These common rituals were spoken transactions, celebrated by the parties themselves; their witness and memory of the events were the evidence that gave the marriage legitimacy. Among Anglo-Saxons, the Beweddung was a public ceremony led by the father of the bride. The groom and his people offered weds to the bride's guardians – guarantees that she would be looked after.

In Scotland and the North of England, couples exchanged vows (plighting the troth) by joining their hands in the handfast. He then called her wyf and she called him husband.

A woman without a guardian – such as a widow – gave herself to the groom. The partners exchanged weds and rings, kissed and clasped hands,

> *In earlier times, the validity of a marriage depended on the consent of the two parties publicly announced or at least symbolised by the exchange of rings or love tokens*

overseen by an orator. The gift by a man to a woman of a ring was popularly believed to imply a formal contract.

Married 'in the eyes of God'

In the 13th century Pope Innocent III declared that the free consent of both spouses, not the formal solemnities by a priest or in church, was the sole essence of a marriage.

A valid and binding marriage was created by a verbal contract, performed by an exchange of vows to this effect between a man and a woman over the age of consent (14 and 12), witnessed by two persons, and expressed in the present tense. A promise in the future tense was only binding if it was followed by sexual intercourse which was taken as evidence of consent in the present.

Married 'in the eyes of God and the Church'

Priests became involved, first as orators to invite witnesses and prompt the vows, later offering the church porch as a place to announce and witness vows made at other public places such as the market cross. Gradually the clergy took over the role of orator, asking those attending whether there were objections to the marriage and then getting the couple to repeat publicly their betrothal agreement which was symbolised by rings and coins placed in the priest's book.

By the 1500s most people brought their vows to church as the final part of the marriage process – the first being the betrothal – and a church service started to take place at the altar rather than in the porch. Although the church did not approve of men and women taking themselves as man and wife before their vows were ratified by the church, since canon law recognised this as the basis of holy matrimony, the church courts

recognised common rites – spousals, handfasts, and trothplights followed by intercourse – as valid marriages.

Marriage and the law

All three branches of the law – ecclesiastical, common and equity – had control over some aspect of marriage. Medieval canon law determined the rules of marriage, they were revised and restated in the Canons of 1604 and enforced by the church courts. The criminal courts could become involved if either party chose to sue the other for a statutory offence such as bigamy. Equity law had jurisdiction over trust deeds and became involved in marriage where there was litigation concerning marriage settlements and the enforcement of trust deeds. The various courts overlapped and contradictory verdicts as to what was or was not a legally valid marriage could be returned.

After inheritance, marriage was probably the single most important method for the transmission of property. As a result much of the litigation about marriage was litigation about property over which the common law had legal jurisdiction.

Uncertain unions and clandestine marriages

By the sixteenth century large numbers of people were living together in situations of varying uncertainty, as there was no consensus about how a legally binding marriage should be conducted. Some – especially the poor – still opted for private verbal contracts, valid in 'the eyes of God', yet often unenforceable in the courts. Others chose a clandestine marriage conducted by a clergyman following the ritual of the *Book of Common Prayer* yet violating canon law in a number of ways, most notably by being performed in private without either the reading of banns or a valid licence from a church official. The advantage of such a ceremony was that the involvement of a clergyman gave it respectability and, most importantly, the marriage was recognised as legally binding having full property rights in common law. There was a huge demand for clandestine marriages as they were considerably cheaper than official church marriages and held in secret – an important consideration for minors who feared opposition from parents or servants who feared dismissal.

The State steps in

By the 1730s public opinion was beginning to turn against the clandestine marriage system with complaints in the London newspapers about the fraudulent seduction of heirs and heiresses. In 1753 Lord Harwicke's Marriage Act, 'for the better preventing of clandestine marriages', stipulated that no marriage other than one performed by an ordained Anglican clergyman in the premises of the Church of England after either thrice-called banns or purchase of a licence from bishop or one of his surrogates was valid. In the case of both banns and licence, at least one party had to be resident for at least three weeks in the parish where the marriage was to be celebrated. Parental consent for those under 21 was strictly enforced. Only the Quakers and Jews managed to have their marriage rites exempted. There were strong objections to the Act – 'proclamations of banns and publick marriages are against the nature and genius of our people' – wrote the *Gentleman's Magazine*.

The continuation of common-law marriage practices

Despite the Marriage Act of 1753 ordinary people still tended to keep marriage informal – many felt that the State and the church had no business in their private lives. One informal ceremony was the Gretna Green wedding. The Marriage Act applied to England and Wales, so crossing into Scotland, where you only had to have your consents witnessed, became popular. As the railways opened up, 'package tours' offering bed and breakfast for 'celebration and consummation' were developed. In Yorkshire, Lancashire and Cheshire those who had gone through some kind of common-law rite were said to be 'married on the carpet and the banns up the chimney' or 'married but not churched'.

In almost every part of Britain the term 'living tally' established itself:
They're livin' tally
They've made a tally bargain
They're noant wed, they're nobit livin' tally

While the origins of the term tally are obscure the term became widespread in the nineteenth century. It conveyed the notion of a definite, if conditional contract or 'bargain', based on the consent of both parties and protecting the women in the case of motherhood. Studies of rural areas have found as many as one in seven couples 'living tally'.

In the mid-Victorian period and throughout the following hundred years common-law arrangements reduced considerably. Since the 1960s a series of administrative rulings, court decisions and laws have given some legal rights to cohabitees, and at the same time the number of couples in cohabiting unions has increased dramatically. These limited rights, however, do not amount to the restoration of the legal recognition of common-law marriage, which ceased definitively with the Marriage Act of 1753.

Sources

1. John R Gillis (1985) *For Better For Worse: British Marriages 1600 to the Present*. Oxford University Press.
2. Peter Laslett (1979) *The World We Have Lost*. Methuen.
3. Laurence Stone (1995) *Uncertain Unions and Broken Lives*. Oxford University Press.

■ This information is produced by One Plus One, the leading relationship training and research organisation. For more information see page 41 for their address details or visit www.oneplusone.org.uk

© One Plus One

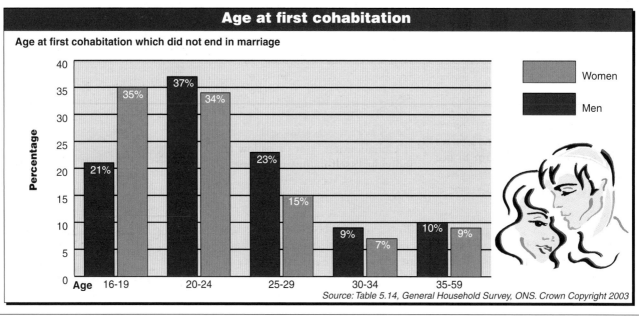

Age at first cohabitation

Age at first cohabitation which did not end in marriage

Legend: Women, Men

Age	16-19	20-24	25-29	30-34	35-59
Men	21%	37%	23%	9%	10%
Women	35%	34%	15%	7%	9%

Source: Table 5.14, General Household Survey, ONS. Crown Copyright 2003

Reasons for cohabitation

Information from CARE

There are a number of reasons repeatedly cited for cohabitation, influencing each couple to varying degrees. One common reason is the fear of divorce, often based on personal experience, or on the experience of the broken marriages of family and friends. This is not just fear of a painful and messy divorce, but also the resulting financial ties, particularly for the man who is likely to have to continue to support his ex-wife and child(ren):

'We both had been married before and we knew of some of the complications that can happen and we just didn't think it was the time to get married. We thought we would wait and see if things would work out.'

A trial run for marriage is an oft-quoted reason for cohabiting. A couple will try out the process of being in love and sexual union, but without the belief that it can necessarily last. Government statistics report that half of cohabitees who perceived there to be advantages in cohabiting mentioned the idea of a 'trial marriage'. Around one-third (30%) mentioned the advantage of no legal ties.

'The reasons given of a trial marriage and no legal ties do suggest the idea of retaining a degree of flexibility, if not freedom, in the relationship.'

Marriage then becomes a ceremony that confirms the partnership:

'We both came from divorced parents. Looking back we realised that they had got married before they knew each other. We decided to live together and see if we really got on well, and learn to live together. We then felt that we could live happily together and then got married.'

Some cohabitees say they can see no advantage in getting married simply to make a cohabiting relationship legal, whilst others are put off by the expense of a wedding. A small number of cohabiting women are opposed to marriage on ideological grounds, believing that marriage is oppressive and restrictive, and that the church ritual and piece of civil paper are meaningless. One in five long-term cohabiting mothers said that they had not married because they were against it.

Half of cohabitees who perceived there to be advantages in cohabiting mentioned the idea of a 'trial marriage'

In general terms, the greater emphasis on individualism as opposed to family values underpins many of these recent family changes. This individualism is closely related to a promotion of self-fulfilment and a rejection of 'traditional' religion. An individualistic ethic encourages us to think egocentrically about relationships (what seems good for me) which is reflected in the expectations many now have of personal self-fulfilment from their relationships:

'Will I find full satisfaction in this relationship?' 'Will my emotional and social needs be fulfilled?' 'If you can't give me what I want then I'll have to look elsewhere.'

Cohabitation seems to allow an individual's self-fulfilment. It appears to offer greater independence, economic control and a retention of one's own identity and image. The attractiveness of cohabitation lies in the lack of legal and other ties, and in the ease of negotiating or separating, should a partner not fulfil one's needs. Some would say, far better the flexibility of cohabitation, should either or both of the partners not be fully satisfied, rather than taking the risk of being tied for life to someone who is 'untested'.

This desire for self-fulfilment may also be reflected in the use of sex for self-gratification: when sex is split from commitment it can become casual and impersonal. The sexual motivation in a relationship can increasingly be one of self-fulfilment and self-gratification rather than one of commitment to and fulfilment of a partner.

'On the one hand (cohabitation) often involves being in love, intimacy, full sexual experience of the partner and high levels of sharing. Each person must open up to the other person and respond to them. But the terms of the relationship are effectively uncommitted ... This is a recipe for hurt, disillusion and hardness.'

There are regular calls to give cohabitation the same status as marriage. However, these ignore the fact that cohabitees have deliberately (if temporarily) rejected the ties of marriage – they have chosen cohabitation because it is different from marriage, because it is easier to walk into and out of and because it appears to give the individual freedom from the responsibilities and restrictions of marriage.

■ The above information is from CARE's leaflet on marriage versus cohabitation and is reprinted with permission. Visit www.care.org.uk for the full document and notes on this text or see page 41 for address details.
© CARE

Alone and never married

More men than women are living the single life

Diary entry for November 7: Calories: 2,500 (pizza and curry). Alcohol: 20 units (10 pints). Weight: 14 stone. Women back to flat: one (mum to pick up washing).

Move over, Bridget Jones, 30-something singletons are much more likely to be men than women. New research from Edinburgh University on the growing phenomenon of solo living has revealed that between the ages of 25 and 44, almost 20 per cent of men live alone, compared to just six per cent of women.

Unlike their female counterparts, the vast majority of them have never been married.

The findings suggest that the media has missed a trick with its portrayal of single women as pioneers of the no-ties life with characters such as Bridget Jones and Carrie Bradshaw of *Sex and the City*. Another Jones film, *Bridget Jones: The Edge of Reason*, opens in Britain this week (7 November 2004).

Adam Smith, one of the authors of the report from the university's centre for research on families and relationships, said: 'We already know that solo living is on the increase and are used to the idea of it being young women. In reality, it is men who are making up most of the single households.'

The reasons for the trend are not clear, according to the researchers. One suggestion is that while Bridget Jones was desperate to find a husband, today's solo-living men are afraid of commitment.

'We don't know if living alone is through choice or necessity,' said Mr Smith. 'Many of these men have never married and could be examples of men avoiding commitment. It could also be a reflection of the demands of careers which take up more and more time and necessitate flexibility.'

Well-documented superior communication skills and the female fondness for intimacy could also mean that more women avoid living alone.

By Julie Henry and Karyn Miller

'It could be that women are more likely to live in shared housing, perhaps clinging on to their student days, and choose to live with one or more friends,' said Mr Smith. 'This would fit in with the increasing number of single people clubbing together so they can afford to buy a place.'

Jason Hart, a 34-year-old graphic designer from Hertfordshire, has lived on his own for six years.

He said: 'I lived in a shared flat when I was a student and didn't really want to go back to that so I aimed to buy a place of my own. I think the benefits are that you can be yourself and you don't have to compromise.

'For instance, the house is quite old and I've done it up myself and it doesn't have central heating. I can imagine that if someone else was here they would be complaining it was too cold.'

Mr Hart said he was happy with his own company and rarely felt lonely. 'I do a lot of stuff and don't spend that much time at home anyway,' he said.

While the stereotype of the bachelor who cannot boil an egg and still takes his washing home to his mother may be outdated, recent research by Warwick University found that living alone was, in fact, detrimental to health.

Bridget Jones's taste for booze and ice cream was mirrored by the study that found that singletons drank more than married people because they socialised more and tended to skip meals such as breakfast or eat on the go.

Tony Reynolds, a 36-year-old website writer who, by his own admission, 'likes a fag and a few pints', said that renting his own flat recently had curbed his excesses.

'I don't know about Bridget Jones but I'm probably more likely to stay in now,' he said. 'I've only had a pint this week, although that could be the novelty of it. I have definitely cut down on takeaways though.'

While the 36-year-old said that he was getting 'too old and grumpy' to have flatmates, he would not rule out living with someone special in the future.

'Good God no. I just think all my male friends who live alone do it through choice,' he said.

'They may be on the look out but they are perhaps more choosy than previous generations who had social pressure on them to settle down. We are fussy buggers.'

Statistics show that almost a third of all British households consist of one person, compared with just three per cent in 1950. About 15 per cent of 30- to 74-year-olds, people traditionally more likely to be married, now live on their own. According to the Edinburgh University study, the trend has significant implications for both the housing market and the welfare state.

Mr Smith said: 'Increased solo living means changing requirements in housing stock, such as the number of homes and their size and rental versus sale.

'It also means that if all these single people do not have children, there will be less family support when they hit old age. This has big implications for social and community care.'

Singletons count the cost of being independent

Over a third of British singletons believe they are penalised financially because of their personal status, according to research from cahoot

Whether it's paying a single room supplement or missing out on sharing the costs of a wedding present, the single life can come at a price. Over a third of British singletons believe they are penalised financially because of their personal status, according to research from cahoot.

Monthly outgoings for a single person can be as high as those for a couple – who have the advantage of sharing household bills. In fact, in a comparison with a couple's monthly household costs, a single person only benefits from slightly lower food bills and a 25 per cent discount for council tax. To help ease the burden of bills, 56 per cent of singletons believe that everyday necessities such as gas and electricity should be offered at a discount to people living alone.

And it's not just house bills that cost single people more. Couples don't tend to spend double the amount on birthday or wedding presents that singletons do, and getting a cab home usually costs the same regardless of how many people share it. Likewise, gym membership often comes with a discount for couples.

Singletons in the 35- to 54-year-old age group are more convinced than the younger generation that they're getting a financial raw deal, as over half said they were being penalised. Younger singletons were less convinced, as only 28 per cent believed they were being punished financially.

Despite the financial penalties, the perception of singletons as the social outcasts of dinner parties and a headache for those planning seating arrangements at a wedding seems to be misplaced. Less than a quarter of those questioned believed there is a social stigma attached to being single in the UK, although this figure was much higher for women between 35 and 44 – 43 per cent of this age group believe they get the social cold shoulder for being single.

The influence of single people in society is set to grow as the number of people living alone is on the increase. Official statistics show that by 2020, one-person households will make up 40 per cent of total households.

Deborah Cutler, Marketing Director at cahoot, said: 'With more people choosing to remain single, not being married with children by the time you're 30 is becoming less of a pressure. However, on the financial side, being single can be a huge burden, with mortgage repayments and utility bills costing roughly the same as a couple, and holidays costing more with single room supplements.'

'There are lots of ways that singletons can save money, such as searching for a lower rate mortgage, credit card or loan, but they can also do little things like clubbing together with other singletons to buy wedding and birthday gifts for friends.'

■ The above information is from a press release available to view at www.cahoot.com

© cahoot

Cost of living

Based on a single person and a couple living in a one-bedroom flat in London, aged late twenties, earning roughly £35,000 each with a £140,000 mortgage, and one car per household. Costs per month:

Description	Single	Couple
Mortgage	£600	£600
Content and building insurance	£25	£25
Council tax	£75	£100
Electricity	£30	£30
Gas	£30	£30
Water	£25	£25
Phone	£30	£30
Sky/NTL	£35	£35
TV Licence	£9.50	£9.50
Car Loan	£150	£150
Petrol	£30	£30
Car insurance	£45	£45
Food/household items	£100	£140

TOTAL	
Single person:	£1,184.50
Couple:	£1,249.50
(per couple member = £624.75)	

BMRB research (12-14 March 2004). Access telephone omnibus survey, interviewing 507 single adults.

© BMRB

Top singleton tips for saving money

- If you've got a spare room rent it out – you'll get extra income and you never know, you might meet your perfect partner.
- Club together with friends to buy wedding and birthday gifts.
- If hosting a dinner party, share the cost. Ask guests to bring a dessert or starter for everyone.
- Don't pay for things like speed dating. Ask friends to set you up with single friends of theirs.
- Get a scooter instead of a car – it's very Continental, will get you round most cities quicker, and is a lot cheaper than running a car.
- Join a gym with a friend to get the couple discount.
- Shop around for the best mortgage, credit card, savings and current accounts and loans and don't be afraid to switch from the bank you've been with for years. cahoot offers a market leading fixed rate loan at 5.9% A.P.R.

Marriage can save you money!

Information from 2-in-2-1

Although the government does little to offer any financial incentive to be married, there are ways in which you can make the most of your married status to make sure that you make the most of your joint income and shared expenditure. Here are just a few.

Make the most of your employment

The first place to look for marital savings is from your employers. Take time to compare closely the benefits you are entitled to for duplication. For example, if your spouse can cover your health insurance, perhaps you can opt for some of the other options such as additional holiday, supplemental life insurance, or medical coverage.

Maximise your relationship with your bank

Banks today offer lots of different bank account options that you can choose (a single combined account; two separate accounts; his, hers, and ours…). Make sure they are linked in the bank's mind so that you qualify for lower fees or higher rates – which usually require a minimum deposit across accounts. Perhaps you could manage with a single account that allows you to write cheques (find one that doesn't charge) and put the extra level of money into a high interest-paying account where you can transfer money at a fixed notice.

Take a look at some of the online banks, which often have lower minimums and may be more convenient for bill paying.

Review your insurances

There are many, many types of insurance, including life insurance, disability insurance, long-term care insurance, health insurance, home insurance, contents insurance, and mortgage insurance. Each comes with variations in premiums, no-claims discounts, protection plans and deductibles. If you haven't updated your policies since getting married or in a long time, take a look at them to see if they fit your current financial state. Some possible changes: maybe you can afford a higher deductible now and can lower your premiums, or maybe with two incomes you have less need for disability insurance.

Although the government does little to offer any financial incentive to be married, there are ways in which you can make the most of your married status

Take a good look at your life insurance, especially if you now have children. Do you have coverage from your employment? Take time to think through the costs of providing full-time care for children in the event that one of you should die, or be incapacitated – the tragedy and trauma will be tough enough, without financial burdens that can't be covered.

Car insurers will often discount your insurance when you get married (especially for young men). Combining car policies together (as well as any other insurance policies) should get you a discount since you will become a bigger (and better) customer to them.

Cut your costs

There is an old adage that two can live as cheaply as one. This is not strictly true but there is a grain of truth in it. You can share the phone line rental bill, the subscription to the paper, and your house, but you still need your own food and clothes! What you can do is take advantage of being a bigger consumer. Buy the litre rather than the pint of milk, the multi-pack of loo rolls, or the caterer's pack of beans!

An environmentally friendly way to cut costs: If you live in/near a town, getting married may mean being able to get rid of one of your cars. Evaluate how often both of you are using a car separately. If it is infrequent, you might be better off just hiring a car for those occasions.

Make some plans

Personal finance and investing are something that you should plan together. Identify the big goals (holidays, cars, ponies, footservants . . .) and talk about your expectations of life together, and the ways in which these things would influence your happiness. Why not prepare a simple budget using one of the readily available home finance packages, or even a simple spreadsheet? Set yourselves some simple targets and watch your savings towards your goals grow!

Find ways to use your complementary skills. Who thinks finding the bargains at the supermarket is fun? Who is more likely to use the coupons that you so neatly cut out of the Sunday paper? Who's better at remembering to pay the bills on time?

If investing and personal finance are new to both of you, why not contact an independent financial advisor? Alternatively take a look at a good book on home budgeting like *How to Get Out of Debt, Stay Out of Debt and Live Prosperously!*

■ The above information is from 2-in-2-1 – see page 41 for their address details.

© 2-in-2-1

Arranged marriage

In the Western world people usually choose their own marriage partner but this is not the way for all cultures living in Western society. Information from YouthInformation.com

Arranged marriages still happen. For example many Indian families who have settled outside India still uphold this tradition. Often the most important aspect is the bond between the two families, rather than the relationship between the couple being married. Property or land with the aim of securing social status sometimes secures marriage agreements.

Supporters of the custom say that divorce rates are lower than among Western society because parents are better able to choose a suitable partner for their children.

The counter argument suggests that the pressure of society as a whole and from the two families concerned keeps the marriage together whether it is successful or not. Divorce therefore is not an option.

Is your family planning an arranged marriage for you?

Many Indian families who have settled outside of India still uphold the tradition of arranged marriage. Being part of two cultures can be hard. Young people born in Britain but from an Indian family can find this particularly difficult if their modern Western lifestyles clash with their parents' hopes and wishes.

Many young Indian people living in Britain know that one day they will agree to an arranged marriage. To deny their parents this would be a sign of deep disrespect. Many families are able to discuss the issue and reach compromises that are suitable for everyone. For example insist that you are happy to meet with prospective partners but that you must like your match. Family friends and relatives will be informed once you've decided to go ahead and soon meetings will be organised. You will be matched in terms of education and experience, a suitable caste, or social class associated with the Hindu religion.

Ideally your partner will be someone with whom you can share interests and who will encourage your

Supporters of the custom say that divorce rates are lower than among Western society because parents are better able to choose a suitable partner for their children

independence. As with any relationship friendship is the key. Good communication from the beginning will help to ensure that yours is a lasting and beneficial partnership.

It is also important to make a clear distinction between arranged marriages that are consensual and marriages that are arranged without the consent of the individuals involved. These are sometimes called forced marriages and are against the law in the UK.

Forced marriages abroad

Are you worried about being forced into a marriage abroad? A small number of young people find themselves being forced into marriage by their families when they go abroad. A marriage should be entered into with the free and full consent of both parties. You have the right to legal protection. If someone is forcing you into marriage they may be in breach of the law in the UK and other countries.

The Foreign and Commonwealth Office is able to help you if you do not want to go through with the marriage. They provide a leaflet with details of how they can help. Contact the Community Liaison Office at the FCO for a copy.

■ The above information is from YouthInformation.com, the online information toolkit for young people from the National Youth Agency. For more information see page 41 for their address details.

© *National Youth Agency*

The truth behind arranged marriages

Striking a balance between society and culture isn't easy. Five young Asians told us how they are adapting the tradition of arranged marriages to suit their modern needs

*By Angela Singh
at Asian Image*

When a new Asian character appears on your favourite soap or film you can bet the issue of arranged marriage is on the horizon. There was *East is East*, where each child was forced to have an arranged marriage, *Coronation Street*, where Sunita fled to Weatherfield to escape hers, and *Bend it like Beckham* where the lead character wasn't allowed to play football or date outside her race.

Although there is a strong stigma attached to Asians and their tradition of arranged marriages, the media stereotypes do not always hold true in this day and age. Arranged marriages always appear forced and against the child's wishes when in fact there often is a choice. 'There's been a shift away from the old trend of arranged marriages where everything was set up and you had no choice,' says Nasser Hanif, a journalist with BBC's Asian Network. Furthermore young British Asian, Salina Arora, firmly believes, 'There are still many modern British Asians who actively seek to find a balance between their culture and modern life.'

So with this in mind *Asian Image* delves into this age-old tradition. We find out why five modern Asian people want or have had an arranged marriage and why they still choose to embrace this tradition.

Jas, 22, an optometry student from Manchester, wants an assisted marriage.

'Marriage isn't on the top of my list at the moment, but I think it will be virtually impossible to meet someone myself as I'm quite shy and busy studying. An assisted marriage, as arranged marriages are known nowadays, would be a great way to meet someone from a similar cultural background who my parents would approve of.

Basically, they would do the research into the family and if they like them they'd exchange photos. It would be up to me to decide if I like the guy and if I want to meet him. After the first date you are free to choose if you want to meet again. Although my parents would arrange the initial meeting, I don't feel much pressure from them as they prefer me to keep both doors open. If I was to meet someone myself then that would be fine but this way I have the backup. There is no pressure as when I meet the guy it is totally up to me.

It would also help as I would prefer to marry a Sikh. My religion isn't my whole life but it is a big part of it. I would want my partner to share in that. There are also fewer divorces with assisted marriages than love marriages.

I don't really believe in all this love at first sight crap and rather than falling in love before, you can fall in love gradually. My parents had an arranged marriage and they were dead against it at first, but once they met they quickly changed their minds and you can see that over the

years they have grown much more affectionate towards one another. I have not met anyone yet, though a few photos have been sent to me so far. I personally prefer to listen to what people say. I want someone who is intelligent with a good sense of humour.'

Anu, 27, a pilot from India, is studying International PR. She had an arranged marriage.

'I went to the USA in 2002 to study, and my parents had set up a meeting with this guy with the potential of an arranged marriage. He belonged to a family that we had known for a long time but I had never seen him before.

When I finally met him, I kept thinking, I might be getting married to this guy, so I was intimidated. But my husband, Rahul, was very casual and we talked about things other than marriage. The second time we met we got engaged, that was in January 2002 and we married in July of that same year. At the time, it wasn't something I wanted to do as I was studying and I wanted to get a job, but I suppose it was meant to happen.

In India, marriage is based on other things besides knowing the guy, we match horoscopes and there are nominations that yes, this marriage will work as well as many rituals. I really believe in them as they tie you together so much that you think this guy is for you and you start to feel it by the time you are married. I was very nervous and scared to begin with as we live in a protective environment and suddenly this man becomes your everything and you don't even know him.

But I do believe marriage changes a lot of things, you don't just get married, you enter into a different family and become part of a different entity altogether. My parents never pressurised me for an arranged marriage but they had their conditions if I found a guy (the caste), so why get involved with a guy your parents will never approve of? This was a life-changing decision, so I trusted their instincts. I am going to join Rahul in December; I have been waiting for this day and I miss him a lot. I am certain things will work out, it may sound like a fairy tale, but I have experienced it.'

Peter, 24, from Preston, is a trainee bank manager. He had an arranged marriage this year.

'When I was 18, I was seeing this English girl and it ended up causing conflict between me and my parents. I was caught up in the euphoria of love and I was blind to everyone else's opinion. I was a really big lad when I was younger and I was insecure about my weight so when this girl took an interest I gripped onto it.

She had been unfaithful to me but I would always take her back because of my insecurity. As I lost weight, people started taking an interest in me and she didn't like this. There were also family differences as my parents would sometimes speak in Punjabi and she thought they would be talking about her. My family always came first and she couldn't understand this. In the end we broke up as we both wanted different things and it was important for me to marry a Hindu Punjabi.

After that Mum and Dad thought I should have an arranged marriage and my grandparents in India knew some people. Initially I dismissed it as I thought I could find someone on my own, but when I saw the picture, I found her attractive. My parents said we'll go to India and I trusted them to know they would have done the research.

In January, we went across and I met her on the same day, it was so nerve-racking. We went to their house; I just sat there until she came in. We went to her bedroom to talk after establishing the formalities; we chatted non-stop for a couple of hours and there was a definite spark between us. Afterwards they asked what I thought of her so there was a lot of pressure.

Although there is a strong stigma attached to Asians and their tradition of arranged marriages, the media stereotypes do not always hold true in this day and age

---

My parents always said that I could say no if I wanted. But after the second meeting there was real chemistry and I followed my instincts, and we decided to get engaged.

The priest decided the day, so nine days after we got engaged, we got married. During the nine days we went to the pictures and got to know each other better. Then on January 26 we got married and I stayed for another seven days.

She's coming to England on May 31 and I am so excited. It's been four months since I have seen her but I phone her twice a day. Although I was scared about marrying a stranger, we aren't strangers anymore. It is going to be incredibly nerve-racking for her as she's leaving her family behind to make a new life so there is a lot of pressure on me.

Obviously we don't know each other inside out but I think it will work as we have a strong relationship over the phone. We're both jokey people and the love is already there. You have to enter this kind of situation with an open mind. I think we will be happy and I have my family to thank for that.'

Ashok, 29, from Nottingham is the brains behind Asian Speed D8 – www.asianspeeddate.com. He also runs his own Stress Management Consultancy in Harlow.

'I got into speed dating as I thought Asians were finding it difficult to meet others. Normally they would rely on their family to introduce them to someone, but in the case of speed dating they are taking the situation into their own hands. At the time speed dating was doing well, so I thought why not set this thing up for them. In this culture there is a lot of pressure to meet someone of the same

---

religion and get married – we please the parents as well as the children.

If you want to meet another Hindu then we provide that opportunity as with Muslims and Sikhs. I think a lot of people marry out of religion due to society, culture and parental pressure and there is a certain degree of pressure from the Asian society.

This isn't an introduced marriage, it is just dating really and the point is to date rather than get married. We have experienced a few success stories with people getting married after meeting at our events and I have met someone too. She turned up late and couldn't date so I chatted to her instead and we've been seeing each other for about a year.

I would personally choose to marry within my culture as I think it is a lot easier if you have certain things in common. I would want to marry someone who is Indian/Hindu as they would understand everything from the religion to the culture, to the food to the language. Nowadays, marriages are not arranged so much as assisted. Your parents introduce you, then you choose who you want to be with – there's a wider spectrum. On one end there is pure arranged marriage and on the other is speed dating. I can't see any drawbacks to speed dating. You meet 30 compatible people from your religion in one evening. The only disadvantage is if you like someone, it's not long enough.'

Aziza, 30, from Blackburn had an arranged marriage 10 years ago. She is still married and has two children.

'I always had an idea I was going to have an arranged marriage. It was part of my culture. It was taboo to talk about boys and out of the question to have a boyfriend, that was the mentality. Although my parents were liberal there was still the Asian community to think of so to bring a male friend home was unheard of.

I did want an arranged marriage as that was the culture and I didn't know any different. It was also important for me to marry a Muslim, I'm not a religious fanatic but I do love my faith.

I was 18 when I met my husband-to-be and he was the first person I was introduced to. I was quite mature for my age and I embraced this type of marriage as my siblings had had them. My parents basically showed me a photo, I liked what I saw, then we were introduced. We didn't go out on dates as such but we met up and we got talking. It was more the personality that attracted me to him.

At the time my husband had come over from India, so we saw each other every day and would look for a house so I got to know him well. When we married I had known him for 18 months. It's not been bed of roses but you have to work at your marriage. When he came over he wasn't fluent in English and vice versa so it was frustrating.

I do wonder what it would have been like not to have had an arranged marriage. But I was one of the lucky ones and we now have two kids. When they grow up I will accept if my girl brings someone home; as time moves on so does your thinking. A lot of my friends have said, "how can you marry someone you don't know and love?", but I got to know him first and love came after.

I don't have any regrets. Had I gone out with someone else, I may have received chocolates and flowers but we've grown to love each other and he's made up for any initial lack of romance.'

■ Reprinted with permission from *Asian Image*, the voice of the Asian community.
© Newsquest Media Group – A Gannett Company (www.asianimage.co.uk)

Significant others

Hollywood couple Will Smith and Jada Pinkett Smith have agreed a pact on extramarital sex. Have they discovered the key to a successful marriage, wonders Stuart Jeffries

Coupledom is a performance art,' wrote the psycho-analyst Adam Phillips. 'But how does one learn what to do together? How to be, once again, two bodies in public, consistently together, guardians of each other's shame, looking the part? Where do the steps come from?' Phillips was not writing about the unconventional marriage of Hollywood stars Will Smith and Jada Pinkett Smith when he wrote these words in his book *Monogamy*, but they are none the less prescient. For Will and Jada have reportedly essayed some new steps to love's old tune: they have agreed a pact that they hope will prevent their relationship from being destroyed by their wandering libidos.

The pact means that either one of them can have sex with a third party so long as the other gives permission. The likelihood of either party granting such permission is, one might think, so low and yet so intriguing that William Hill might think of opening a book on it. 'You don't avoid what's natural,' Will Smith reportedly said. 'You're going to be attracted to people. In our marriage vows, we didn't say, "Forsaking all others".'

Will has apparently admitted to Jada that he has sexual feelings for other women, an admission that does him much credit, though one that will surprise no one but the most dry-balled old monk. When he was working on the film *Hitch*, for example, he described his co-star Eva Mendes as 'freaking gorgeous'. If Jada has any sense, she will forgive him everything but the use of the word 'freaking'.

The monogamous strictures underpinning marriage have long been derided as bourgeois by voguish lefties keen to get laid

If all this is true, the couple, probably unwittingly, have recognised another of Adam Phillips's apercus: 'You can't be monogamous and unfaithful at the same time.' Instead, they would appear to be trying for a third way between monogamy and infidelity – one that involves being faithful to one's married partner while allowing a kind of extramarital sexual licence that will not be allowed to destroy the relationship. Three words: good freaking luck. Only a cynic would argue at this stage that this pact is likely to be as successful as that other third way, though it is too early to say that the couple has found the formula for a happy marriage.

Will argues that, should he feel impelled to consummate his hypothetical dalliance with some supposition of a hottie, he will say to Jada: 'Look, I need to have sex with somebody. I'm not going to if you don't approve of it – but please approve of it.' Again, Jada might well take particular exception to one word in that sentence: the unctuous 'please'. When a man pleads for sex it is never particularly edifying; when he pleads to his wife for sex with a third woman, she would be justified in grabbing him by his sticky-out ears and nutting him into the middle of next week.

But do open marriages ever work? Anecdotal evidence is not conclusive either way. *Monty Python* comedian Terry Jones, for example, was for 34 years in an open marriage with Alison Telfer, but when she learned of his affair with a 22-year-old Swedish student before Christmas, she asked him to leave the marital home.

On the other hand, Tom Conti, the actor noted for playing the Greek waiter Costas who said to Pauline Collins's Shirley Valentine, 'I want a to make-a da fuck with you', has, according to an interview his daughter Nina gave to the *Mail on Sunday* last November, been in an open marriage for many years. One can only hope that nubile Swedish students and Conti's own importunate filmic overtures don't ruin his conjugal felicity.

The monogamous strictures underpinning marriage have long been derided as bourgeois by voguish lefties keen to get laid. Both Simone de Beauvoir and Jean Paul Sartre described their open relationship in philosophical terms. They claimed they had a lifelong 'essential' relationship, but continued to see other people in 'contingent' relationships. Perhaps this contingent-essential distinction is the one that Will should try on Jada if the need arises. Frida Kahlo and Diego Rivera also had an open marriage premised on a socialist rejection of a bourgeois institution: that is why she had sex with Trotsky and other women without the Mexican muralist being able to complain. Though if he wasn't white-hot with jealousy, surely something had died in their relationship.

Perhaps monogamy is, given the nature of sexual desire, hopeless. Deborah Anapol, a California-based psychologist and author of *Polyamoury: The New Love Without Limits*, believes so: 'It seems clear that without some major renovations, marriage is doomed. If the new paradigm for love can save marriage from the scrap heap, so much the better.' When so many marriages end in divorce, she seems to have a point.

But is Anapolian promiscuity the answer? Like monogamy, one might think it is a perilous affair, but only multiplies the opportunities for jealousy, hurt and intra-relationship headbutting. Adam Phillips wrote: 'Profoundly committed to the better life, the promiscuous, like the monogamous, are idealists. Both are deranged by hope, in awe of reassurance and impressed by their pleasures.'

Perhaps the idealism, both of monogamy and its seeming opposite, promiscuity, is what needs to be ditched. Instead of idealism, realism. This, surely, is what Joan Bakewell was talking about when she said that her marriage to Michael Bakewell had 'mutually acknowledged infidelities'. Bakewell, the TV presenter whose seven-year affair with Harold Pinter inspired his play, *Betrayal*, understood that those affairs eroded marital trust – a realisation that Will and Jada are yet to experience. 'Yes, of course one did mind about the infidelities in the end,' she has said. 'Our marriage was as human and muddled and awkward and jealous and full of attempts to understand as human life itself.' This humble thought certainly seems more plausible than trying to hermetically and self-defeatingly seal oneself from the perils of desire – though it hardly guarantees (what could?) a happy marriage. Instead of being deranged by hope, we need to rearrange our expectations.

Maybe these considerations are beside the point for Will and Jada. They have been married for seven years, and have a family to support. He has a new single to promote and a film to plug. What better way to do so than for the couple to give interviews that guarantee acres of prurient coverage and big pictures? For Hollywood stars, coupledom is probably even more of a performance art than we have hitherto recognised.

Bridget Jones generation is single . . . and proud of it

Britain's growing band of Bridget Jones singletons are happy to keep it that way, according to a new report

More than half of single women were 'very happy with their lives as they are', compared to 46 per cent of men.

The survey for Valentine's Day of 1,039 people also found one in four men aged 25 to 40 lives with their parents, compared to 13 per cent of women. About 46 per cent of single men said they were 'very happy with their lives as they are', against 56 per cent of women.

Jenny Catlin, a consumer analyst at Mintel, said: 'Women seem more independent than men and able to cope better with single life. These women seem to really enjoy the sense of achievement they get from coping with problems on their own, much more than men do.'

The survey also found both women and men are becoming less interested in marriage, with 28 per cent of women and 19 per cent of men saying they have 'no wish to be married or to live with someone'.

Peter Kearney, a spokesman for the Scottish Catholic Church, agreed that young people did have less inclination to marry.

He said: 'The state has a role in helping people prepare for marriage. At present, it is easier to get a marriage licence than it is to get a driving licence.'

By Michael Blackley

The report found that three in ten single men aged 25 to 40 see 'not having enough sex' as the main disadvantage of not living with a partner, although 23 per cent also miss the comfort of being given a hug.

Some 36 per cent of women of this age see the main disadvantage being the assumption of others that they want to be in a relationship.

> **About 46 per cent of single men said they were 'very happy with their lives as they are', against 56 per cent of women**

Professor Alex Gardner, a clinical psychologist in Glasgow, said attitudes towards sexual relationships had changed for a number of reasons.

'It used to be that women gave sex for companionship and men gave companionship for sex,' he said. 'But now, in modern society, with the increasing use of contraception and more relaxed moral demands, women are able to have sex when they want.'

The Scottish author Jenny Colgan said that women have moved on and often find their network of friends more important than having a partner.

'Men don't have the same emotional support as women do, and they never really open up to friends in the same way,' she said.

'The idea of the Bridget Jones culture and women sitting getting drunk on their own is a bit passé,' she added. 'If anyone's sad enough to wake up with a tear in their eye this morning, then there's as much chance of it being a man as there is it being a woman.'

■ This article first appeared in *The Scotsman* on 14 February 2005.

Wedding rings: a brief history

The wedding ring is for most people the most public sign of their commitment to each other. The continuous circle of the ring symbolises a never-ending love. It was believed by ancient Egyptians that the third finger on the left hand was directly connected to the heart by one vein; hence it was seen as the perfect finger for a wedding ring. The Romans are said to have introduced the custom of wearing a wedding ring to Britain.

Rings were made from hemp or rushes or even a lock from your loved one's hair in ancient times, however today they are made from more durable materials; 18-carat gold is most commonly used, although some couples opt for white gold, red gold or platinum rings.

In some European countries, the ring is worn on the left hand before marriage, and is moved to the right hand during the ceremony. The earliest engagement rings were also used as wedding rings, sealing the act of transference of ownership of a daughter from father to husband.

National Marriage Week

Marriage Week 2005 (7-14 Feb) claims that unmarried parents are five times more likely to break up than married parents, and that married couples should be able to transfer their tax allowances

National Marriage Week 2005

2nd February 2005: Marriage Week 2005 will be launched at the Jubilee Room, Palace of Westminster, Monday 7th February, 11.30 am. Speakers at the Press launch include Jonathan Sacks, Annette Brooke MP, Liberal Democrat Children's Spokesperson Andrew Selous MP and Harry Benson, Director of Bristol Community Family Trust, who will say, 'Britain's unmarried families are collapsing, three-quarters of all family breakdown with young children now involves unmarried families, it is now no longer plausible to argue that all relationship types are equal – the evidence is irrefutable.'

Richard Kane, Director of Marriage Week, will say, 'Government policy pretends that all family structures are equal. Whilst all relationships are valuable, some are more valuable than others. Government policy should incentivise commitment through taxation and increase funding for marriage support programmes'.

Marriage Week 2005, which is welcomed in messages of support from Tony Blair, Michael Howard and Charles Kennedy, as well as Rowan Williams and Jonathan Sacks, reflects activity occurring throughout the UK as churches and other community groups host events which are designed to enrich the relationships of those attending.

Marriage Week suggests that any couple can enrich their relationship by learning about each other and by applying specific tactics, which will build love, passion and commitment. New research suggests that women will generally commit at the point of 'moving in', whilst men tend to withhold commitment until a marriage ceremony, which would help to explain the appalling level of breakdown amongst unmarried families. During the Press launch two

recently married 'real' couples will be interviewed about their experience of 'learning love' and commitment through taking part in relationship skills courses.

Family structure

Family stability varies a great deal depending on whether parents are married or not.

Numerous studies show that cohabiting couples are far less stable than married couples (e.g. Marsh and Perry, 2003; Boheim and Ermisch, 1999). Nearly one in two unmarried parents will have split up before their child's 5th birthday compared to one in twelve married parents (Kiernan, 1999). More recent data from the Millennium study confirm this discrepancy in stability between married and unmarried parents (Kiernan, personal email communication).

Divorce rates may not have changed much in 25 years. Yet during this same period there has been a huge national trend away from marriage. 5% of births in 1960 were to unmarried mothers, 12% in 1980 and 41% today (ONS, 2004). By combining data on births with data on break-up rates, I can estimate the annual number of children under five whose parents split up. An astonishing 75-80% of all family breakdown with young children now involves unmarried parents.

Child outcomes

A recent study of 36,000 US families (Brown, 2004) was the first to compare outcomes amongst children from cohabiting and married biological parents as well as cohabiting and married step-parents. The study found that primary school children from unmarried families tend to do worse at school, although their well-being depends more on economic and parental resources. Secondary school children from unmarried families tend to do worse behaviourally and emotionally. However, there were no differences in outcomes

between children from single-parent families, stepfamilies or either type of cohabiting families. The conclusion is that not only does it matter that children live with both parents, it matters that their parents are married.

Selection or relationship effect

Researchers and policymakers have debated for years whether the benefits and protections found in married families are the result of selection (people who do better get married) or relationship (people who get married do better). A number of recent well-designed longitudinal studies strongly suggest the presence of a relationship effect. Selection is no longer an adequate explanation.

Getting married significantly reduces rates of depression whilst moving in together does not. Whether people are depressed has no influence on the odds of getting married in the first place (Lamb et al, 2003).

A seven-year study ruled out the possibility that lower rates of alcoholism amongst married compared to cohabiting women – and depression amongst men – were due to selection effects (Horwitz et al, 1996).

Getting married significantly reduces rates of depression whilst moving in together does not

---

The difference in relationship quality between couples who did or didn't cohabit before they got married in the 60s/70s was often explained away as a selection effect. However, the continued presence of similar differences amongst couples marrying in the 80s/90s, when cohabitation became more commonplace, argues instead for a

relationship effect (Kamp Dush et al, 2003).

A study of 3,000 low income families found that family breakdown was significantly more likely amongst cohabiting parents, even after taking hardship and other economic factors into account (Marsh and Perry 2003).

Taken from a paper prepared by Harry Benson Bristol Community Family Trust for the 2nd National Conference on Relationship Education, London. 9th February 2005.

Notes

Office of National Statistics, New Marriage figures released 9am Friday 4th February 2005.
The average taxpayer pays £570 on the direct costs of family breakdown and just 21p on prevention.

■ The above information is from a press release provided by Futureway, the organisers of National Marriage Week – see page 41 for address details.
© Futureway

With this prenup I thee wed

A new report calls for premarital contracts to be made legally binding in English courts. There's a surging demand for them, says Clare Dyer – and not just from movie stars

Steve and Imogen signed their prenuptial agreement on the steps of Chelsea register office just minutes before they took their marriage vows. Last week they celebrated their 13th wedding anniversary. They're glad they haven't had to invoke the agreement – which spells out what should happen to their assets if they ever divorce – but are reassured that, if the need arises, it's there in a bottom drawer.

At the time they were pioneers. Even today, while prenups are widely used in the US and continental Europe, relatively few British couples take the precaution of signing on the dotted line before they plight their troth. After all, prenups are not legally enforceable in our courts.

That could change if the government takes up a recommendation from the largest group of specialist

family lawyers in Britain, the Solicitors' Family Law Association (SFLA). In a new report, the association calls for premarital agreements to be made legally binding in England and Wales unless to enforce them would cause 'significant injustice' to husband, wife, or any children of the family.

The move, the association believes, could prevent many of the costly and damaging divorce battles which now see warring couples' assets depleted by huge legal bills. The wide

discretion enjoyed by judges in England and Wales (it's much less in Scotland) makes it difficult to predict what a court might decide and therefore hard to negotiate out-of-court settlements.

The uncertainty, lawyers believe, plays a big part in the bitter divorce property fights which regularly hit the headlines. In the latest, boatbuilder Charles Currey last week (24 November 2004) lost his appeal against a ruling which let his heiress ex-wife stay in the £1.5m family home from which he once ran his business, while he had to leave. He had been awarded £640,000 to buy a new home but had already spent £350,000 battling with his former wife before he was ordered to pay the full costs of the failed appeal as well.

In recent years the judges themselves have moved the goalposts. First, they decided there should be a 'yardstick of equality', valuing a wife's years spent looking after the home and children just as highly as a husband's efforts in creating the family wealth – though not necessarily awarding each equal shares in the carve-up. Then, in the case of footballer Ray Parlour and his ex-wife Karen, they decreed that some of the future earnings of a highly-paid husband could be brought into the pot.

'The way English law currently operates is fairly random, possibly counter-intuitive and certainly unexpected for many people,' notes Steve. He was an investment banker of 37 when he suggested to PR executive Imogen, also 37, that they should sign a prenup. They knew it might not be enforceable in court but both took legal advice to make sure it was as watertight as possible in case they ever needed to call on it.

'We were both financially independent, both had jobs and had acquired independent levels of assets,' Steve explains. Each had a flat and the agreement spells out that if the spoils of their joint life have to be divided, Steve will keep what belongs to him while Imogen retains what's hers.

Some see prenups as the triumph of pragmatism over romance, but Steve disagrees. Their legal document is evidence, he says, that he and Imogen wanted to marry 'for reasons of the heart, not for financial reasons'. Two years after the wedding, they bought a house together and had to update their agreement. Both now 50, they have no children,

Family lawyers say the publicity over celebrity prenups seems to be prompting more clients to ask for them

although their lifestyles have changed over the years. While Imogen still runs her PR business, Steve now writes articles about art history and earns much less than he did 13 years ago.

Though the prenup was Steve's idea, Imogen readily agreed. 'People who ask "Why on earth would you have one?" tend to be left-wing feminists,' she says. 'I'm surprised by that because they're the last people I would expect to think I'd marry a man for his money. We've put it away in a drawer and forgotten about it, like Catherine Zeta-Jones said she did.'

For rich international celebs such as Zeta-Jones and husband Michael Douglas, the prenup is as vital a part of the wedding preparations as the exclusive photo deal with *Hello!* or *OK* magazine. But family lawyers say the publicity over celebrity prenups seems to be prompting more clients to ask for them. And, although they are not legally binding, the few cases which have gone to court show a growing willingness among judges to give them significant weight.

In a landmark case in 2002, a deputy high court judge largely enforced a prenup signed on the eve of marriage by a north London

property tycoon thought to be worth up to £150m and his pregnant wife-to-be, who had no job but a £1m trust fund from her father. She was awarded what she had signed up to in the agreement – a lump sum of £120,000 after a two-year marriage and a London home which would revert to her ex-husband when their son grew up. All she got on top of the agreement – which gave her no right to maintenance payments – was £15,000 a year to run the house.

Legally binding prenups are common in Europe and the US, and Australia passed a law in 2000 making pre-marriage agreements enforceable. So why not here? The idea was floated in a government consultation paper in 1999, which argued that it could reduce the scope for conflict on divorce and give people more control over their own lives. By providing more certainty about what would happen on divorce, an enforceable prenup might actually encourage people to marry rather than just live together, the paper suggested.

The proposal got nowhere at the time, largely because the high court family division judges were less than enthusiastic. They wondered whether agreements might precipitate couples into divorce by conditioning them to the idea that their marriage might fail. Some judges felt the move would devalue the institution of marriage. The majority suggested that prenups might be given 'greater prominence' in divorce cash battles, but only a minority would go further and make them enforceable – provided, in the

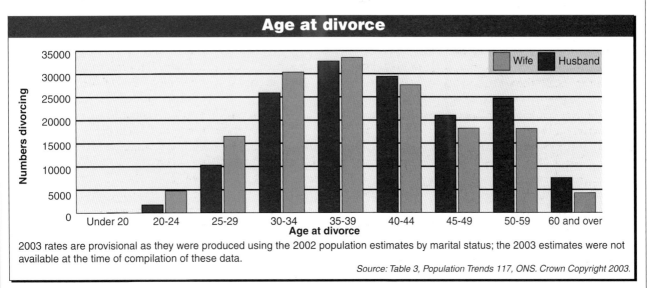

Age at divorce

2003 rates are provisional as they were produced using the 2002 population estimates by marital status; the 2003 estimates were not available at the time of compilation of these data.

Source: Table 3, Population Trends 117, ONS. Crown Copyright 2003.

individual case, that this would not conflict with the interests of any children or plainly cause injustice. Five years on, with the retirement of some of the more traditionally-minded judges and an influx of new blood into the family division, that minority might now be a majority.

With the growing trend for courts in England and Wales to take premarital agreements into account, lawyers are seeing a surge in demand for them. 'While prenuptial agreements are not legally binding here, they can be highly persuasive in determining the award by the court,' says Ann Northover of the Mayfair law firm Forsters. 'Recently clients from "old money" families have been entering into these agreements in an attempt to protect family trusts and inherited wealth. The same applies for exceptionally wealthy entrepreneurs.'

Nor are prenups just for the rich. When so many couples delay marriage until their 30s and when more people are marrying for the second

How to make it stick

The courts are more likely to take a prenup into account if:
- Both parties had independent legal advice
- Both made full disclosure of their financial positions to each other
- Neither party was under pressure to sign
- There was a 'cooling-off' period of a month or so between signing the agreement and the marriage
- The couple's circumstances have not changed significantly since the agreement was signed. If they do change – the birth of a child is an example – it should be updated.

or third time, with children from earlier unions whose inheritance they want to preserve, the trend is trickling down the income brackets.

The idea of legally binding prenups seems to chime with government plans to try to help separated couples sort out their own disputes over their children, reducing hostility and saving on legal aid. The SFLA argues that reducing the scope for litigation over money too should 'promote conciliatory divorce and encourage positive relationships between children and parents who separate'. And the family assets needed to fund two homes would have more chance of being preserved, rather than being depleted by costly legal battles.

- 'A More Certain Future: Recognition of Premarital Agreements in England and Wales'. Summary on the SFLA website at www.sfla.org.uk. The names Steve and Imogen are pseudonyms.

© Guardian Newspapers Ltd 2004

Pre-nuptial agreements

Information from DivorceUK

What is a pre-nuptial agreement?

In simple terms it is a written contract between parties who are about to get married. The contract terms are intended to bind the parties to a certain future course of action. Most people would assume that the intention is to avoid one party claiming 'family money' from the other party in a divorce. However, it could be a very useful means of avoiding possible conflict on other matters e.g. if a couple come from mixed religious background or different countries it could lay out the intention regarding religion or education of children.

A pre-nuptial agreement cannot attempt to override the laws of the country e.g. you could not have a clause preventing one spouse from applying to the child support agency. Thus, the terms should be reasonable

and put against the context of local laws. Otherwise, the courts, if it comes to that, will not uphold the contract terms. Here are some pros and cons.

Pros and cons

FOR:
i. It can record each party's financial standing at the outset of a marriage which could be a very useful reference point in a later separation dispute
ii. It can bring clarity to many 'debatable' points between the parties e.g. the type of wedding desired, religion and education of future children, including or excluding lifestyle issues e.g. golf no more than once per week
iii. It can keep the future 'in-laws' happy, if there is concern about financial imbalance between the parties.

AGAINST:
i. Even raising the issue of a pre-nuptial with your partner may put a strain on the relationship
ii. Is it really necessary as you may find that the law already covers what you are trying to deal with?
iii. Do not assume that the court will enforce the terms particularly when trying to avoid normal financial settlement terms.

What to do next

If you are thinking about entering into a pre-nuptial agreement we recommend that you use our Pre-Nuptial Agreement pack and have the terms checked by a specialist family lawyer.

- The above information is from www.divorceuk.com

© DivorceUK

24

www.independence.co.uk

The dinner party verdict: don't panic about marriage

Yvonne Roberts joins an eclectic mix around Michael Portillo's table and hears an optimistic take on relationships

A cartoon in the *New Yorker* shows two men drinking in a bar. 'So,' one says to the other. 'How's the family? Still disintegrating?' The cartoon appeared more than 30 years ago but, if recent divorce figures are any guide, the meltdown in relationships continues unabated, as does the search for causes and cures.

According to right-wing critics, marriage is not only being smashed on the rocks of selfish individualism but also drained of all meaning by the increase in same-sex partnerships and the rising numbers of couples drifting aimlessly into cohabitation only to split apart again almost immediately – all to the detriment of children.

To consider these and other questions linked to the future of the family in the twenty-first century, Michael Portillo, Conservative MP for Kensington and Chelsea and rapidly emerging on TV as a Tory

Rudolph Valentino with brains, recently invited half a dozen guests to the Carlton Club in London for his BBC4 series, *Dinner with Portillo*. I was there.

The guests included Martin Reynolds, a gay cleric; Baroness Uddin, a Muslim Labour peer married at 16 and still married after 27 years; Fiona Millar, partner of Alastair Campbell and chair of the National Family and Parenting Institute; Alain de Botton, philosopher, husband and soon-to-be father; Anne Atkins, a wife and mother of five and an anti-divorce, anti-abortion agony aunt; and the liberal and married Bishop Stephen Venner .

Half an hour into the conversation, a slightly frustrated Portillo, presumably expecting more dissent, taxed his guests. 'Who on earth is going to run up a flag for marriage? The priest won't do it, the philosopher won't, the Muslim won't, the bishop won't, the politician won't.'

In truth, the bishop, among others, had provided an eloquent defence – backed by the fact that almost 60 per cent of married couples are predicted to remain together, contrary to the pessimistic portrayal frequently drawn in the media.

Cohabitation too, a notoriously fragile partnership, is also beginning to change. Among the better educated, longevity is slowly becoming more common. Millar has lived with Campbell for more than 24 years, has three children and has no urge to marry. 'It's important not to forget that there are many people out there who have fairly conventional families who may not be married,' she said.

Reynolds also believed he was part of a 'good' family. His physically disabled mother lives with him and his gay partner of 25 years and their handicapped foster child, while an aunt acts as housekeeper: 'It's a model extended family.'

While divorce may have risen among twentysomethings, the trend is for couples to wait until their early thirties before tying the knot. The older the bride and groom, the better the marriage's chances of survival – not least because the couple have roamed around enough to realise the grass probably isn't greener elsewhere.

This delay in becoming a bride, however, may be less to do with a contemporary desire to live a life first, and more a result of that traditional dilemma – the absence of Mr Right. 'Highly educated Muslim young women, who are fantastic and bright, just can't find compatible husbands,' Uddin said.

Portillo concurred. 'I see a lot of people in their twenties who are immensely stressed about the fact that they haven't found a partner.

They experience a great deal of loneliness and, this may seem very old-fashioned, but they reach their late twenties and think they are never going to find the person of their dreams.'

Perhaps that explains the hike in twentysomething divorce figures. They can't find the man of their dreams, so they settle for the bloke who turns out a bit of a nightmare.

In the recent past, of course, 'commitment' was reinforced by social convention. Women remained at home, which meant many had neither the money nor the opportunity to philander. Divorce also carried a stigma, so tearing a family in two often meant shame, exile, destitution.

Nowadays, while social pressure to stay together exists in ethnic communities, what keeps other couples together – through the bad times, as well as the good? Or, as de Botton put it more bluntly – why bother? A question especially pertinent in a workaholic, time-squeezed society with a 30-second attention span and a compulsion to consume the latest shiny object of desire – even if that's your best friend's spouse?

'What happens,' de Botton asked the bishop, 'if someone says: "Actually, I think I'm going to be happier with multiple partners, shifting around. I don't really believe in this effort?"' In an era of ecclesiastical relativism, the bishop's reply proved refreshingly unequivocal: 'Fulfilment as an individual in isolation is a contradiction in terms. It's impossible. We find fulfilment with others, it's a voluntary undertaking to try to develop a relationship that is going to be fruitful for yourself, for your partner, for the family and the wider community.'

Love, of course, isn't meant to be about hard work. For twenty-somethings, in particular, such utilitarianism just isn't what they call romance. Once upon a time too, everyone knew their matrimonial role. Now negotiations are trickier, so while the theory of what the bishop is saying is impeccable the practice is obviously proving a great deal more fraught.

Somewhere around the pudding, a new consensus began to emerge – although one not endorsed by

---

For increasing numbers, the search for love and its consequences has an added dose of realism

---

everyone. Since political engineering to make marriage more attractive via, for instance, tax incentives has patently proved less than successful, why not put the children first and focus government support on trying to encourage better parenting by putting someone else's interests first?

Good enough parenting, we are told, is defined as including, among other qualities, fairness, consistency, affection, honesty, trust, reliability and an investment of time. In short, much the same ingredients that also improve our chances – whether gay or heterosexual – of staying together.

Atkins and Portillo, natural Tories (although Portillo now professes to be in favour of divorce and contraceptive and abortion advice for vulnerable 13-year-olds), appeared wary of encroaching on what they see as private family business.

'If you look at the twentieth century, bad parenting may have done all sorts of bad things but interventions by the state have been really evil,' Portillo said.

His view was challenged by Millar: 'It's not an intervention, it's helping people. The answer surely is to help parents to develop all these characteristics that we know help children to become secure and healthy, mentally and physically, from a very early stage.'

By the coffee, we still lacked a perfect union of minds. Is the family in transition or decline? Are we fashioning a modern definition of commitment or each going our separate ways? And what kind of price, if any, will our children pay?

If you listen to the doom-mongers, women in their twenties in particular are fleeing the matrimonial coop, barely before the bridal dress is out of the dry cleaners. Latest statistics reveal that among 25- to 29-year-old females, marriages are breaking up at the rate of almost 29 in every 1,000, double the national average. Marriage break-ups rose by 5,755 in 2003, reaching 153,490, the biggest annual increase since 1985.

So are we destined to become a nation of singletons, heading for a lonely old age in a society with little sense of community? Or do many of us prefer going solo – the first generation to view long-term commitment as a positive impediment to living in a happy, healthy, fulfilled household unit of one?

According to Ivor Frones, a Danish sociologist, who has tried to find some answers, the myth of Cinderella and her prince endures – but, for increasing numbers, the search for love and its consequences has an added dose of realism.

'We may still entertain the idea that somebody's foot fits the glass slipper,' he says. 'But we also know that happiness is no longer something you find: it is something you achieve.'

■ This article first appeared in *The Observer.*

© Guardian Newspapers Ltd 2005

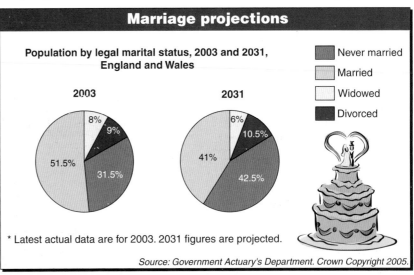

Marriage projections

Population by legal marital status, 2003 and 2031, England and Wales

2003
8%
9%
51.5%
31.5%

2031
6%
10.5%
41%
42.5%

Never married
Married
Widowed
Divorced

* Latest actual data are for 2003. 2031 figures are projected.

Source: Government Actuary's Department. Crown Copyright 2005.

Divorce

Information from Resolution

Sadly, every year around 150,000 marriages end in divorce. The legal process of ending a marriage can have a major impact on all family members – both emotional and financial. Recognising this, Resolution members aim to help separating couples achieve a constructive settlement of their differences in a way which avoids protracted arguments and promotes co-operation between parents in decisions concerning children.

If you are having problems in your marriage, you should first consider whether these difficulties could be resolved with the help of a trained relationship counsellor. Organisations such as Relate could help you – see their website at www.relate.org.uk

If you decide to divorce, a solicitor will be able to advise you and guide you through the process. A good lawyer will outline your options at every stage and give you the information to make your own decisions.

To get a divorce in England and Wales, you need to show that you have been married for more than a year and that the marriage has broken down. The marriage must have broken down for one of the reasons below:

- Your spouse has committed adultery and you find it intolerable to live together;
- Your spouse has behaved in such a way that you cannot reasonably be expected to live together;
- You have been separated for 2 years and your spouse agrees to divorce;
- You have been separated for 5 years;
- Your spouse deserted you more than 2 years ago.

The reason for the breakdown of the marriage forms the basis of the divorce application (known as the 'petition'). If more than one of these is applicable, your solicitor will advise on which is most suitable to your circumstances and what additional information the court needs.

If your spouse has committed adultery, you do not need to name the other person. If the petition is based on the behaviour of your spouse, you will need to give some limited examples of their behaviour and how it has affected you.

These details (known as 'particulars') can be agreed with your spouse in advance, to avoid the process of untangling the marriage increasing any conflict between you both.

If you carry on living together for more than six months after either the last act of unreasonable behaviour or the discovery of the last act of adultery, then you cannot get a divorce based on this. Similarly, a period of separation is discounted if you live together again for a period of six months.

The divorce process is in two stages – a 'Decree Nisi' and a 'Decree Absolute'. A Decree Nisi is an interim stage, granted by the court when the ground for divorce is established. After a period of time, it can be converted into a Decree Absolute, which marks the end of the marriage. This will not normally happen until arrangements for any children and financial matters are agreed. You can stop the process at any time before the Decree Absolute is issued.

If you have children, you will need to give details of their names and dates of birth of the children, where they are living, which schools they attend and what arrangements have been made for their care – see our factsheet on 'Arrangements for children after divorce or separation'.

You will also need to settle financial matters relating to the family home, maintenance, pensions, and any savings and investments. The legal term for this is 'Ancillary Relief' – see our factsheet on 'Financial arrangements on divorce'.

The time it takes to get a divorce will vary according to the complexity of each case and the practice of the particular court. Even the most straightforward divorces will take between four and six months.

■ The above information is from Resolution, first for family law. For more information see page 41 for their address details or visit the website www.resolution.org.uk.

© Resolution

Legal jargon for divorce

As if you haven't got enough to deal with, you have all these obscure words to try and decipher. Welcome to TheSite's legal phrasebook and translations

TheSite.org

Separation

■ **Separation Agreement:** document setting out the terms agreed, usually before divorce proceedings are considered.

■ **Judicial Separation:** a formal separation sanctioned by the court that enables the courts to make orders about money and property.

Divorce

■ **Petition:** the document by which a divorce or judicial separation is applied for.

■ **Answer:** the formal defence to a divorce petition.

■ **Request for Directions:** application to the court for a decree nisi.

People involved

■ **Petitioner:** the person who applies for a divorce or judicial separation.

■ **Respondent:** the other spouse upon whom the divorce or judicial separation proceedings are served.

■ **Co-Respondent:** a person with whom the respondent is alleged to have committed adultery. The law no longer requires that person to be named as a Co-Respondent in the divorce proceedings.

■ **District Judge:** a County Court judge who deals with most of the divorce proceedings and usually with financial matters.

Finally

■ **Decree Nisi:** the provisional order indicating that the court is satisfied that the grounds for divorce have been established.

■ **Decree Absolute:** the final order of the court, which brings the marriage to an end.

■ **Property Adjustment Order:** an order that a husband or wife should transfer property to the other.

■ **Clean Break:** a financial arrangement where it is agreed or ordered that the husband and wife will make no further claims against each other for capital or maintenance.

■ **Consent Order:** an order made by a court giving effect to the terms agreed between husband and wife.

■ The above information is from the website www.thesite.org.

© *TheSite.org*

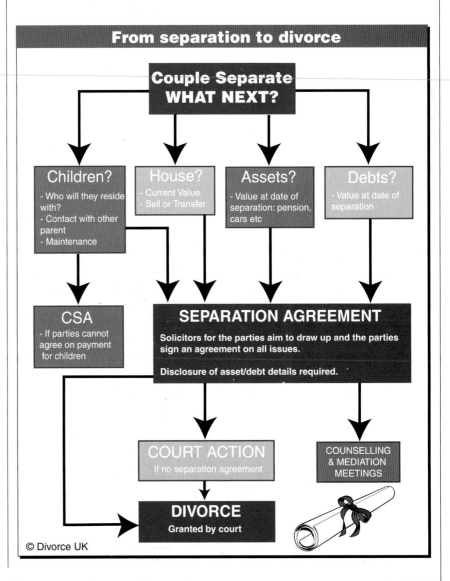

From separation to divorce

Couple Separate WHAT NEXT?

Children?
- Who will they reside with?
- Contact with other parent
- Maintenance

House?
- Current Value
- Sell or Transfer

Assets?
- Value at date of separation: pension, cars etc

Debts?
- Value at date of separation

CSA
- If parties cannot agree on payment for children

SEPARATION AGREEMENT
Solicitors for the parties aim to draw up and the parties sign an agreement on all issues.

Disclosure of asset/debt details required.

COURT ACTION
If no separation agreement

COUNSELLING & MEDIATION MEETINGS

DIVORCE
Granted by court

© Divorce UK

Why relationship support is important

Information from 2as1.net

It is not difficult to understand that healthy relationships – and the love and support involved – are an important component of a healthy society. As the Government said in its 1998 Consultation Paper, *Supporting Families*:

'Strong stable families provide the basis for raising children and for building strong and supportive communities', and 'this Government believes that marriage provides a strong foundation for stable relationships'.

But it also recognised that 'there are strong and mutually supportive relationships outside marriage and many unmarried couples remain together throughout their children's upbringing and raise their children every bit as successfully as married parents'.

Couple relationships are important in their own right, but many couples also become parents or provide elder-care. The quality of the parents' relationship is central to their children's well-being, but is not the only factor.

There is a significant correlation between parental experiences and the outcomes experienced by children once they reach adulthood. In general, children brought up by birth parents experience the lowest levels of conflict and early difficulty. Children brought up by two birth parents until the age of 16 have higher levels of life satisfaction and more family support, fewer psychological problems and less conflict at every age.

But it is important to emphasise that family relationships are complex. Most outcome research is based on 'historical' samples, and may not be directly applicable to contemporary families, where divorce is more commonplace; negative outcomes for children are particularly associated with damaging unresolved family conflict; and most children thrive after a period of adjustment following separation, divorce and loss.

Relationship instability among adults is an increasing feature of modern life, and the ending of some relationships may improve the quality of life for those individuals and their children. Nevertheless, it makes sense to aim to provide a network of support for people who need help to work through difficulties.

Adverse effects of divorce, separation and relationship breakdown on couples, children and the taxpayer

'When relationships break down, the physical and emotional costs can be high. There is a link between relationship breakdown and poor physical and mental health.'

Adverse effects are many and varied:

On couples

In the longer term, more people are likely to be affected as they get older and face age and infirmity alone.

'Less easily quantifiable costs associated with the negative effects of ongoing relationship conflict for self-esteem, health and productive capacity. The indices of these costs are to be found in stress-related claims made by adults and children on health, social and psychological services, and in some absenteeism at work.'

On children

Parental conflict is an important influence in a number of adverse outcomes for children in both intact and separated families.

There is a greater probability of poor outcomes for children from separated families than others.

The outcomes for children who have experienced disruption and multiple family structures are generally worse than for those living continuously with a lone parent or stepfamily.

Constant changes to residence or contact arrangements have been shown to have a negative impact on children. A 'bad' divorce or relationship breakdown is therefore particularly likely to affect children adversely, and also affect their ability to make and manage relationships and to parent successfully in the future.

On society and the taxpayer

Family breakdown and divorce impose a huge cost on the taxpayer. Hart, in 1999, estimated it at about £5 billion a year. This was based on evidence from the House of Commons Library in July 1994, which pointed to annual costs (in 1993-94 prices) of social security benefits (£3 billion), social services (£80 million), legal aid (£266 million), health (£190 million) and other costs. Other commentators have suggested that the costs are much higher. But this is a difficult area to quantify precisely.

The effects of conflict

Disagreements between parents are a normal and necessary part of family life. Most children are unaffected by their parents' arguments. (Indeed, children may be harmed if parents' ill-concealed attempts to suppress anger create a silently hostile environment.) However, children who grow up in an atmosphere of extreme marital discord are likely to develop emotional and behavioural problems.

Couples argue in different ways. It has been suggested that some types of conflict are more harmful to children than others. Destructive conflict is particularly detrimental to children's well-being. This type of conflict is characterised by verbal or physical aggression, non-verbal conflict (the 'silent treatment'), intense quarrels, and arguments that are concerned with or involve the children. (Even children as young as one and two have been found to become distressed when observing parents quarrelling.) However, children may learn from observing constructive conflict, whereby parents effectively manage and resolve disagreements. Similarly, children may learn from productive conflict where problems are openly discussed but not necessarily resolved.

Links between marital conflict and children's difficulties appear to be stronger in families experiencing multiple problems. Parental depression and family stresses, such as socio-economic pressure and work stress, may increase the likelihood for discord, as well as further reducing parents' ability to engage positively with each other and their children. On the other hand, if parents are able to respond supportively to one another during periods of family stress, they may reduce the risk of harm to the child and provide helpful models for handling future stress.

Children as young as one and two have been found to become distressed when observing parents quarrelling

---

Stresses imposed by parenthood can provoke or intensify discord between parents. This discord, which is often associated with postnatal depression, may ultimately have serious consequences for the well-being of the couple and their children. So learning to resolve conflict constructively, and being supported to do so, can have a very beneficial impact on all concerned.

Adverse effects of domestic and family violence on couples, children and the taxpayer

It is not known how many separations and divorces are precipitated by family violence. The effects of family violence on parents and children are well documented, though costs to the public purse are less clear.

However, on any day in the United Kingdom, around 2,500 women, plus their children, are in refuge accommodation after fleeing domestic violence.

In nearly one in five counselling sessions held in English Relate centres on 28 September 2000 (over 900 in total), domestic violence was mentioned during the counselling session as an issue in the marriage.

In Greater London, the estimated cost to the public sector of responding to domestic violence is £278 million each year.

In providing relationship support, it is therefore vital that there is no diminution of support for men, women and children fleeing violence or abuse, and no increase in the difficulties they face in achieving protection through separation or divorce.

■ The above information is from 2as1 – see page 41 for address details.
© 2as1.net

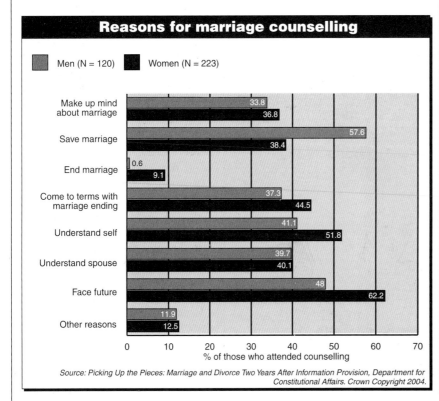

Reasons for marriage counselling

Men (N = 120) Women (N = 223)

Reason	Men	Women
Make up mind about marriage	33.8	36.8
Save marriage	57.6	38.4
End marriage	0.6	9.1
Come to terms with marriage ending	37.3	44.5
Understand self	41.1	51.8
Understand spouse	39.7	40.1
Face future	48	62.2
Other reasons	11.9	12.5

% of those who attended counselling

Source: Picking Up the Pieces: Marriage and Divorce Two Years After Information Provision, Department for Constitutional Affairs. Crown Copyright 2004.

Rise in divorces is blamed on the web

Labour under fire over biggest increase in break-ups since 1985

Last year saw the biggest increase in divorces in two decades.

Marriage break-ups rose by 5,755 to 153,490 in 2003 – the third successive annual rise in a single year since 1985.

The divorces left another 153,527 children under 16 in broken homes.

And it put the divorce rate, which is calculated by the number of break-ups for every 1,000 couples, at 13.9 – closer than ever to the all-time high of 14.3 recorded in the early 1990s.

The counselling group Relate blamed the surge on Internet websites such as Friends Reunited which encourage old flames to meet up again.

'Websites and chatrooms make having an affair easier and are among a whole host of reasons for the rise in divorce rates,' spokesman Christine Northam said last night (August 31 2004).

'The first relationships we have are often very powerful and if we are feeling miserable we may be tempted to go to Friends Reunited to see what an old boyfriend or girlfriend is doing now.

By Steve Doughty
Social Affairs Correspondent

'If you're feeling wobbly in your relationship you may look back to a more rose-tinted past.'

The Office of National Statistics said last year's 153,490 divorces was a rise of 12,390 on the 2000 figure of 141,100 – despite a drop in the married population.

If the divorces continue to rise, the number could eclipse 1993's all-time peak of 165,000.

Some critics say the Government is also partly to blame because it is stripping away the legal and moral authority of marriage and offering couples growing financial incentives to steer clear of getting wed.

For example, the abolition of tax breaks such as the Married Couples' Allowance means there are few legal and financial privileges for the married. And Gordon Brown's flagship tax credits are aimed at helping single people.

The effect is that many couples with children are actually better off divorcing and living apart than staying together.

Analyst Robert Whelan, of the Civitas think-tank, said Tony Blair and his ministers were ignoring proven links between the decline of marriage, the collapse of the family, poverty, crime and social breakdown.

'All academic research shows divorce is closely connected to social breakdown and crime,' he added.

'Crime and anti-social behaviour gets worse when families break down or fail to form and there are no fathers to instil civilised behaviour in young men.'

But he added: 'The Government will do nothing about this. It views marriage as no more than a lifestyle choice. It doesn't want to know about the damage divorce and the failure of the family causes.'

The average divorce now comes after 11.3 years of marriage, up from 11.1 years in 2002.

Women aged 25-29 are most likely to divorce, with more than a quarter in every 1,000 splitting up with their partners last year. On average, women are 39 when their marriage ends and men are 42.

In the early 1960s, before legal reform and the sexual revolution took effect, there were just 25,000 divorces a year.

By the mid-sixties, there were nearly 40,000 a year, rising to 127,000 in 1971 after the 1969 law reform introducing 'quickie' divorces.

In the early 1990s, the number rose again. But it declined towards the end of the decade – partly because the falling popularity of marriage meant there were fewer couples to break up.

■ This article first appeared in the *Daily Mail*.

© Associated Newspapers 2004

For first-time losers in love, life starts again at 50

Forget all the talk about life beginning at 40 because it is 50 when it really starts

By Sarah Womack
Social Affairs Correspondent

Hundreds of thousands of men and women in their fifties are having to look for love again, often after decades with one partner, according to new research.

Intriguingly, most say they are still looking for the 'loves of their lives', even though the majority have been married before. They believe that their fifties are the best time to look for a partner; their reminiscences of teenage dating are that it was universally 'awful'.

The research among 300 women and 200 men aged 50-70, was conducted by the website Friends Reunited Dating, a sister site of Friends Reunited. One in six people registered on the dating service are over 50, up from one in 10 last year.

With the forthcoming royal wedding shining a spotlight on 'later love', the research offers an insight into what it is like to look for a companion in late middle age.

Rhoda Moore, of Friends Reunited, said: 'Growing older clearly does not stop people continuing to look for the great loves of their lives. The golden age of dating actually starts when you reach 50.'

According to the Office for National Statistics, increasing numbers of women are finding themselves alone in middle age as a result of rising divorce figures.

There are now almost two million people over 50 who divorced between 1998 and 2000.

And in an unprecedented demographic shift, the number of young people is dwindling while the older sector of the population rapidly expands.

By 2025 more than a third of Britain's population will be over 55. Researchers predict that the baby boomer generation will revolutionise what it means to be old because their attitudes are so different to those of their parents.

More than half (54 per cent) of men and women over 50 say that they consider kindness to be the most important factor when looking for a date, says Friends Reunited Dating.

Perhaps unsurprisingly looks are more important to men (22 per cent of them rate appearance as important) than to women (nine per cent).

Eight out of 10 men and women say they use online dating 'because it is harder to meet single people as you get older'.

> *More than half (54 per cent) of men and women over 50 say that they consider kindness to be the most important factor when looking for a date*

Like most dating agencies and websites, people use them for different reasons. Almost half are looking for 'fun', because they are single, divorced or widowed. The other half say they are looking for marriage.

Whether it is fun or marriage, most say they are still looking for the love of their life (men 84 per cent, women 78 per cent), and want respect, civility and gentleness.

Age Concern said there was a time when people who were bereaved or divorced would accept that situation for life, but the mindset had changed.

'Many older people are dating, travelling, returning to university or continuing their careers,' said a spokesman.

'They are enjoying living life to the full and meeting new people and having new relationships as part of a positive approach to life.'

© *Telegraph Group Ltd, London 2005*

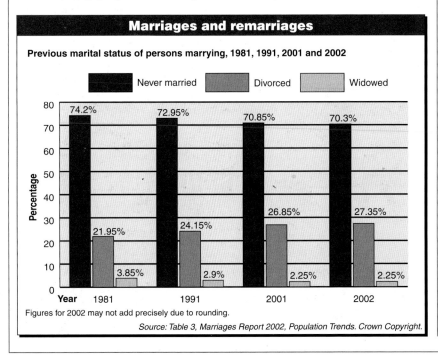

Marriages and remarriages

Previous marital status of persons marrying, 1981, 1991, 2001 and 2002

Never married | Divorced | Widowed

Year	Never married	Divorced	Widowed
1981	74.2%	21.95%	3.85%
1991	72.95%	24.15%	2.9%
2001	70.85%	26.85%	2.25%
2002	70.3%	27.35%	2.25%

Figures for 2002 may not add precisely due to rounding.

Source: Table 3, Marriages Report 2002, Population Trends. Crown Copyright.

Divorce through the eyes of a child

Information from Divorce.co.uk, run by Mills and Reeve

How children see things

Because children see things differently to adults, it is helpful to understand what they may be going through. They will hurt, they will feel pain, sadness and loss. They may also be angry.

Limiting the damage of divorce for them should be your aim.

Unless there is violence or abuse, children will want to maintain as good a relationship with both their parents as possible. This is backed up by the law, and courts will promote this wherever possible.

From a growing body of research, a child's initial responses to his or her parents' marriage breakdown are likely to include the following:

- children feel shocked, bewildered and lonely when they actually hear the news that their parents are separating or divorcing;
- most children would prefer their parents' marriage to continue although most have at times considered the marriage to have been unhappy;
- research tells us that 5-6 years after a divorce only a small number of children think that their parents were wrong to have divorced;
- often children do not understand why their parents have split up;
- children feel sad and anxious at the possibility of losing touch with the parent who is leaving;
- children do not know whether the separation is temporary or permanent, which adds to their bewilderment. Being bewildered threatens a child's sense of security;
- many children fantasise about their parents getting back together – even after long periods after separation;
- however little the parents know of the future, the children know even less;

MILLS & REEVE

- children and parents give strikingly different pictures of their feelings and of their understanding of the reasons for separation;
- all children will feel upset, even if they do not say so and even if they do not show it.

How divorce affects children

Children of different ages will react in different ways; however, it is helpful to understand all of them if you are a parent splitting up.

How divorce affects pre-school children

At around two months after separation, both boys and girls often become frightened and confused; they may also become clingy. They may start behaving immaturely, going back to patterns of behaviour they had grown out of.

They may become aggressive, especially boys. Boys particularly may seek out male attention and affection. Because they can become aggressive and confrontational, children can become isolated and shunned by other parents or by their friends.

A child's distress feeds on the mother's distress and vice versa. It can be a vicious circle of painful feelings when the family splits up. Young children of this age are not yet mature enough to know how to understand, control or voice their feelings.

How parents can help

As well as talking to children simply and repeatedly about the separation, parents need to try if possible to keep with the family rules and routines. It is tempting for parents to relax the rules in these circumstances, but that may well make children feel less secure. On the other hand, suddenly becoming harsh and disciplinarian – which is likely when a parent is feeling overwhelmed by the experience of separation – will make children more anxious or frightened.

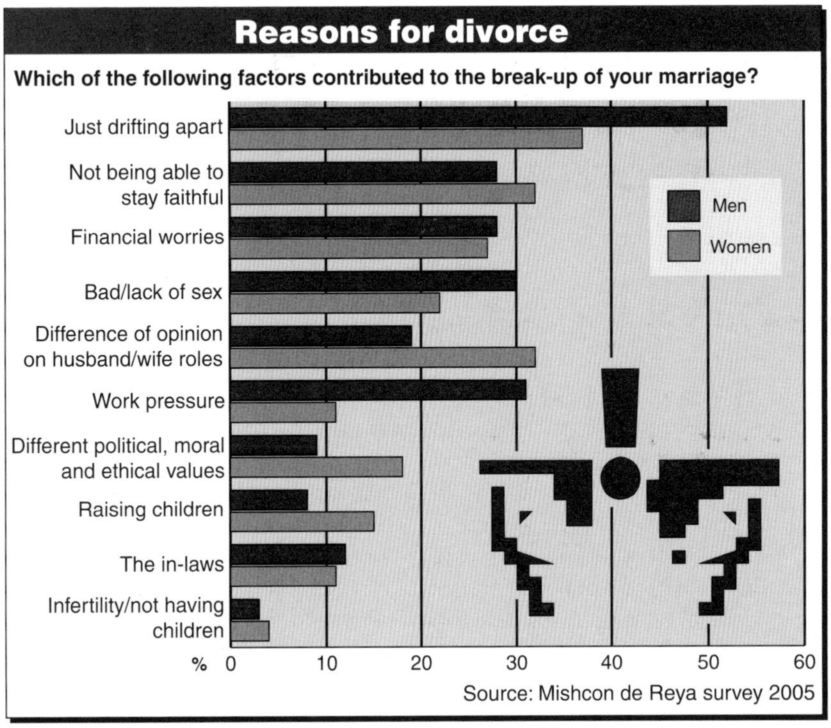
Reasons for divorce
Which of the following factors contributed to the break-up of your marriage?
Just drifting apart
Not being able to stay faithful
Financial worries
Bad/lack of sex
Difference of opinion on husband/wife roles
Work pressure
Different political, moral and ethical values
Raising children
The in-laws
Infertility/not having children
Men
Women
% 0
10
20
30
40
50
60
Source: Mishcon de Reya survey 2005

How divorce affects children from 6 to 9

Crying and sadness characterise children in this age group. Missing the departing parent is the most dominant concern of children of this age, and although it is shared with children in the younger age group, it is more likely to be spoken about. Boys often 'act out', and show signs of aggression.

Children of this age may also begin to express guilt, as if it is their fault that the marriage is ending. Similarly, this age group may openly urge their parents to get back together.

How parents can help

Although it is difficult for parents, it is healthy to allow children to cry and mourn the loss of the family as they knew it. Glossing over the sad feelings may make a child feel bad or even strange for having those feelings. If the child is encouraged to disown the sad feelings, then this may lead to resentment or withdrawal from the parent concerned.

Simple phrases like 'I understand how sad you are at what is happening' or 'everyone feels sad at this time' can be very powerful in helping your child accept his or her very normal and inevitable feelings.

Parents need to tell children that it is not their fault.

Parents of this age may find an explanation helpful, in very simple terms, of why the marriage came to an end.

How divorce affects children from 9 to 11

This is the age at which children often become intensely angry with their parents' divorce. They may blame the parents or even reject one of them, most commonly the parent with whom they live. Boys are more likely to become aggressive whilst girls are more likely to become withdrawn. School performances are often affected as well.

How parents can help

As well as the advice from the previous sections, it is important that parents accept that their children will be angry. This acceptance will help to disperse the child's feeling of impotence over an event they do not want to happen. Tolerating anger which may seem arbitrary and unconnected is the most helpful way of managing these feelings.

These feelings are often expressed in the place children feel most safe and to the safest person.

How divorce affects adolescents

Adolescents also get angry and feel pain at the loss of a family they have known. Because they feel more adult, they may assume adult-like responsibilities and concerns. For example, they may express worries about the future of the family or the well-being of younger siblings.

The danger of a child assuming such adult-like burdens is that his or her own feelings of sadness and concern are glossed over; they feel unsupported and even emotionally abandoned.

This can lead to anger, particularly in boys, and withdrawal, especially in girls.

Older adolescents also tend to take refuge in sexual relationships, with research showing that the children of divorced parents tend to marry younger (and so are more likely to divorce themselves).

Adolescents do have a greater ability to communicate their feelings and this can mean a stronger bond with the parents during this stressful time. Sometimes, an adolescent can develop a better individual relationship with a parent once the atmosphere of tension or conflict is reduced.

School performance often diminishes and can lead to dropping out early from the educational path.

How parents can help

Although it easy to be persuaded by a child's apparent ability to help and understand, adolescents still need parents to parent them.

These children are the ones most obviously caught in the middle, because they become the confidants of one or both parents and feel forced either to take sides or to engage in a constant test of loyalty. Teenagers need to be free of this difficult position. It is important for them to have their say, but children even of this age cannot be expected to exercise adult judgement over the long-term effects of choosing their social lives over seeing their other parent, for example. Parents need to take a long-range view for them, and ensure that they maintain that relationship with the other parent (unless violence or abuse indicates otherwise).

■ The above information is from the website www.divorce.co.uk.

© *Mills and Reeve*

Together and apart

Children and parents experiencing separation and divorce

Concern about divorce and separation is partly fuelled by the rise in the divorce rate and the numbers of children affected by family changes. There is also growing concern about the role of fathers and the need for children to maintain a good relationship with both their parents. Recent years have seen the development of a growing range of services designed to help children and families experiencing these changes.

The Joseph Rowntree Foundation has supported a collection of research projects on children's and parents' experiences of separation and divorce. These studies have examined the outcomes for children of changes in their family circumstances, and what can help them at these times of stress. The research reports have also looked at the experience of separation for those who have been cohabiting as well as those who divorce, and at the impact of separation and divorce on fathers, as well as on mothers and children. Mavis Maclean, of the University of Oxford, summarises this research here.

- Researchers suggest the need to see parental separation not as an event but as a process which begins long before a parent departs and continues throughout childhood. They stress the importance both of making sure that children are told clearly what is happening and of listening sensitively to what children have to say about decisions which affect them.
- Separation for children can be particularly difficult when followed by a number of other changes to the family setting, for example where parents find new partners or where new children are brought into the household.
- Financial hardship and parental distress are also associated with continuing problems for children.

JOSEPH ROWNTREE FOUNDATION

- Formal interventions need to be child-centred and available to all on the basis of need rather than civil status. However, many children seek better communication with and informal support from friends and family.
- We need to move on from seeing the children of divorced and separated parents as having an experience which is essentially different from that of other children. All children experience a number of transitions that can be difficult for them, and for which they may require additional support.
- A poor relationship between the separated parents is understood to add to the difficulties in establishing successful arrangements for contact between the child and the non-resident parent. However, there are also many practical issues that concern families on separation. Considerations such as housing and working hours can also be barriers to developing and maintaining contact.

The policy landscape

In *Supporting families*, the first Green Paper on the family published by the Home Office in 1998, the Government set out as its mission statement: 'The interests of children must come first'. At a time of increased incidence of separation and divorce, it is important for parents to be able to care for their children even when they do not share a common household, to be able to adjust to periods of lone parenting, and to cope with new family structures when mothers and fathers form new partnerships and other children are brought into the household as either step- or half-siblings.

The policy goals set out in *Supporting families* aim to support parents undergoing family change in a number of ways. These include involving wider kin networks, improving advice and information services including financial advice, seeking a better balance between the demands of home and work, and supporting adult relationships. Marriage is seen as the preferred setting for bringing up children but, in the interests of the children, parenting in other settings is to be valued and supported.

The policy landscape is changing rapidly. In September 2003 the Government published a Green Paper, *Every child matters*, following the inquiry into the death of Victoria Climbié. In his foreword, the Prime Minister emphasises that 'for most parents, our children are everything to us'. The paper proposes strengthening both universal services, such as schools and health and social services, together with targeted

The figures

The divorce rate rose rapidly between the mid-1960s and mid-1990s reaching 161,000 in 1997 and subsequently levelling out below 150,000 a year. Two-thirds of those divorcing, and an unknown but substantial number of those who separate after living together, have children under 16. It is more difficult to be precise about the numbers of separating cohabitants as the end of their relationship is not recorded in any public document.

specialist services for children needing additional support. Planned legislation will create Directors of Children's Services, accountable for educational and children's services as part of 'children's trusts'. A Minister for Children, Young People and Families has been appointed, and there are proposals for a new Children's Commissioner. This legislation and ministerial change only affects England; Wales already has its own Minister responsible for children and young people and a Children's Commissioner. The new Minister in England is consulting on the extent to which the Green Paper will apply to frameworks already in place.

The policy issues

Important policy questions have been challenging Government, voluntary organisations and those working with families. These are:

- Are children negatively affected by separation or divorce; if so, which groups of children?
- It is generally agreed that it is important for children to maintain their relationship with both parents. But, how important is it that a non-resident parent has contact with their children when this is not welcomed by the parent with care nor by the children, or where there are questions about inadequate parenting or domestic violence?
- How should we support parents both before and after they split up in their parenting roles and in dealing with the problems of parenting after divorce?
- How can such help be best delivered to parents and children?

Recent policy developments

Attempts to encourage widespread use of mediation in divorce though the Family Law Act of 1996 failed. Subsequent government responses have been to pilot the idea of a 'one-stop shop' for advice. The Family Advice and Information Network (FAIN) will initially be based in solicitors' offices. In addition, the Government has tried to strengthen the Children and Families Courts Advice and Support Services (CAFCASS), to make it a broad-ranging advice service not focusing solely on divorce or other disputes. However, this has not yet been considered to be successful. Moving CAFCASS from the former Lord Chancellor's Department to the Department for Education and Skills may be helpful.

Findings from the JRF Programme

The findings from JRF research in this area throw light on these policy areas, and in particular on what needs to be considered in helping parents and children at times of family change.

- From the *Findings: Together and apart: Children and parents experiencing separation and divorce* published in 2004 by the Joseph Rowntree Foundation. Reproduced with permission. See page 41 for contact details.
© The Joseph Rowntree Foundation 2004

A focus on family change

Divorce or separation is only one of a number of changes to their family life which children undergo. New partners for either parent may have children already. There may be children from a new relationship, and there may be subsequent separations and other new partners. It is clear that multiple transitions, however well-handled, are difficult for a child to cope with. Interventions by Government or professionals can no longer focus on a single event, but need to support children throughout the many changes which take place in the course of family life.

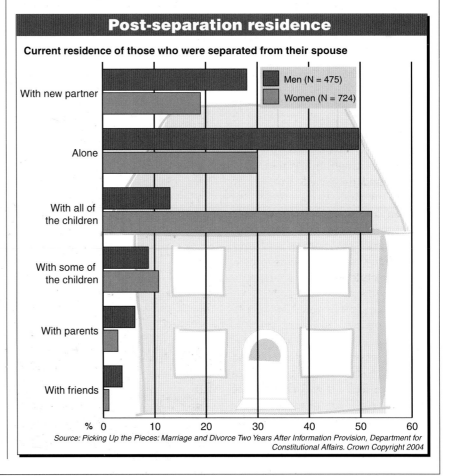

Post-separation residence

Current residence of those who were separated from their spouse

Men (N = 475)
Women (N = 724)

With new partner
Alone
With all of the children
With some of the children
With parents
With friends

% 0   10   20   30   40   50   60

Source: Picking Up the Pieces: Marriage and Divorce Two Years After Information Provision, Department for Constitutional Affairs. Crown Copyright 2004

How to be a good parent after divorce

Information from FamilyOnwards

Many couples who separate tell each other that whatever happens 'the kids will come first'. Their intention is right and praiseworthy but saying it is much easier than actually carrying it out.

To allay the children's anxieties the usual answer is to tell them that, 'Although Daddy and Mummy can't live together, we both love you.' Is this the end of the story? No, unfortunately it is just the beginning.

Of course, in the best of all possible worlds, the rules for a smooth family transition would mean that everyone would be polite, considerate, they would always be on time for collection and pick-up, and there would never be a cross word in front of the kids. It is an ideal which many parents strive for, but as the saying goes, it takes two to tango. And parents who are totally out of sync with each other are unlikely to be able to negotiate this difficult step satisfactorily.

Even if a couple – let's call them Jane and Jim – decide that they will do all in their power to see that the kids don't suffer, how is it that the relationship can turn so sour and that all too often children find themselves caught in the middle?

Jane and Jim decided that they would, in their words, *divide the children up* ... so that Ben and Holly would swap over homes every week. 'After all,' they agreed, 'didn't "everybody" say that this is what is best for children after a divorce?' What seems to have escaped them is that unlike the material household goods, the bank accounts and the pets, all of which can be divided up without answering back, Jane and Jim overlooked the fact that the kids will have feelings and thoughts of their own. They were genuinely puzzled when after a few months the children were showing signs of distress: 'It seemed to be working so well,' they said. It had, in fact, worked *for them* but they had not thought to discuss the matter with the children!

Many parents are unable to curb their own feelings so that all the grief and hurt they feel pours out onto the child

---

What about a couple who are at war from day one? When one partner feels betrayed the temptation is to hit back, and what often comes to mind is to 'punish' the other parent either by making access difficult, or to engage in bad-mouthing the parent who has left. I am not talking about a systematic brainwashing. Very few parents would resort to 'Parental Alienation Syndrome' which is what the experts have termed the deliberate attempt to poison a child's mind and attitude towards a parent. What is much more prevalent, and often unconscious, is a constant putting down of the other parent, by constantly referring to how 'Your mother never . . .' or 'How I wish your father . . .' This can and does affect the child adversely.

Sadly, many parents are unable to curb their own feelings so that all the grief and hurt they feel pours out onto the, often bewildered, child. Veiled messages are sent from parent to parent through the kids, which is just not fair. Barbara: 'All I did was tell Robbie to ask his dad to buy him new trainers. That caused a terrible row, but I can't afford to buy everything Robbie needs and his dad needs to know this.' As a result of this message Jim shouted at Barbara for 'spoiling his day with his son' and Barbara shouted back that there was not enough money to go around, let alone go to Legoland. Was it really any surprise that Robbie was distraught, thought it was all his fault

that his parents were shouting at each other, and was too poorly to go to school next day?

When there is another person, perhaps a new lover, on the scene, the complications multiply. Often in the throes of a new love a parent is excited and wants to include the child in the new relationship, but this is more than likely to cause much fury and misery to the parent left behind. Lily: 'I feel that Tammie has taken over my husband, my life, and now she wants my kids. No!'

Often finance and access get confused: 'I won't pay if you won't let me see my kids.' 'Remember, you left us. We are not going to make it easy for you. They don't want to speak to you on the phone.' The battles rage, and again the kids suffer.

So what about our couple – Jane and Jim – who began with high hopes and thoughtful planning? Family therapy sessions showed them how

> ## *You may, or may not, have had a choice about the breakup of the family, but remember the children never have that choice*

far apart they were in their parenting ideas, and how this had affected their children. Jane: 'We understood good intentions weren't enough. We were four people who had to find a new way. We couldn't do it in theory, it needed to be by trial and error. At the beginning we comforted ourselves by saying the children would be okay. Of course they were not. We think we have it right now – or as right as it can be after the breakup of a family.'

A last word from Angie: 'I know the theory. Kids need both parents, but it's hard, very hard. Any arrangements we do make get broken at the

last moment. I am the one to pick up the pieces. We started off trying to be friends, but there is too much water under the bridge and now we are not speaking. My heart bleeds for the children.'

I think Angie truly sums up the difficulties of parenting after divorce. Of course there are guidelines, and many compromises have to be made if parenting is to be top of the agenda. All too often it slips down the page as fury, retaliation, and pure bloody-mindedness are what get to the top.

You may, or may not, have had a choice about the breakup of the family, but remember the children never have that choice. I am afraid they are nearly always caught in the crossfire of parents at war.

■ Information from FamilyOnwards – see page 41 for contact details.

Mediation and you

Mediation helps those involved in family breakdown to communicate better with one another and reach their own decisions about all or some of the issues arising from separation or divorce – children, property and finance

Mediation is about directly negotiating your own decisions with the help of a third party. It is an alternative to solicitors negotiating for you or having decisions made for you by the courts. Entering mediation is always voluntary.

How does it work?
A trained mediator will meet with you both for a series of sessions in which you will be helped to:

■ Identify all the matters you wish to consider
■ Collect the necessary information
■ Talk about the choices open to you
■ Negotiate with each other to reach decisions that are acceptable to you both
■ Discuss how you can consult your children appropriately about arrangements.

What does the mediator do?
The mediator's job is to act as an impartial third party and manage the process, helping you to exchange

information, ideas and feelings constructively and ensuring that you make informed decisions. The mediator has no power to impose a settlement – responsibility for all decisions remains with yourselves since you know better than anyone else what is right for your family. The mediator will not advise you about the best option either for your children or your financial affairs, nor can the mediator protect your individual interest.

Will I still need a solicitor?
YES. You will need a solicitor to advise you on the personal consequences for you of your proposals. You will be encouraged to engage a solicitor whom you can consult during the mediation process. At the end of mediation your solicitor will be able to advise you about your proposals and translate them into a legally binding form.

Will we have anything in writing?

At the end of mediation you will usually have achieved a written summary of the proposals you have reached. This is not a legally binding document and you will need legal advice about it especially if you have reached agreement on financial and property issues.

How much will it cost?

Each Service has their own scale of charges. They will also be able to advise you if you are eligible for legally aided mediation, which is free.

Is mediation suitable for everybody?

Sometimes mediation is not the best way for you to resolve your problems. You will have a chance to discuss this in more detail at your first individual meeting with the mediator.

Is mediation confidential?

Firstly mediation is confidential and courts are also likely to regard the discussions as privileged.

Confidentiality – The Service will not voluntarily disclose to outsiders any information obtained in the course of your discussions without first obtaining your permission (unless it appears there is a risk of significant harm to adult or child).

Privilege – What you say during mediation cannot be used later in court as evidence. But facts disclosed during mediation are regarded as

open information and although strictly confidential may be used subsequently in court.

Will the mediator talk to the children?

In mediation you are regarded as the experts on your children and will have valuable knowledge and information about their needs, wishes and views. However there may be times when you both would like the mediator to consult directly with the children about your plans. In those circumstances children would be asked for their specific comments and views on your joint proposals, without having to take sides in any difference of opinion between their parents.

Such a meeting needs careful planning and is confidential in so far as the mediator and children agree what the mediator will say to the parents after the meeting.

What are the benefits of mediation?

Research conducted by the Joseph Rowntree Foundation with Newcastle University identified that three years later couples felt that mediation had helped them to:

■ End the marital relationship amicably.

■ Reduce conflict.

■ Maintain good relationships with their ex-spouses.

■ Carry less bitterness and resentment into their post-divorce lives.

Couples felt that mediation had helped them to . . . carry less bitterness and resentment into their post-divorce lives

---

■ Be more content with existing childcare arrangements and less likely to have disagreement about child contact.

■ Be able to reach agreement that had survived the test of time.

■ Be glad they had used mediation.

Source: Family Mediation

■ The above information is from the Divorce Online website at www.divorce-online.co.uk

■ Families today have a variety of different labels, including 'traditional', 'step', 'blended', 'child-free', 'gay' and 'one-parent'. (page 2)

■ Only one-fifth of households are made up of a married couple with dependent children. (page 2)

■ The median duration of marriage for couples divorcing in 2000 was 11 years. (page 3)

■ Eighty-eight per cent of stepfamilies consisted of a couple with one or more children from the previous relationship of the female partner. (page 3)

■ A One Plus One study of marriage in the early 1980s showed that the attractiveness of marriage lay partly in the fact that it provided a 'package of rights', guaranteeing immediate transition to adulthood. Today, it is more socially acceptable for couples to begin a sexual relationship, set up home, and have children outside formal marriage. (page 4)

■ Research at One Plus One has found that many factors inspire newlyweds to marry – a gradual feeling of disillusionment about being single, fears of growing old alone, and perceptions that they were now 'ready' for marriage. (page 5)

■ Wives – and husbands – who divorce have a right to claim maintenance, a lump sum, and a share of any family property, even if it is in the other partner's name. Cohabitees who split up have no such rights. (page 7)

■ The number of cohabiting couples is predicted to soar from two million today to 3.8 million over the next 25 years. (page 7)

■ A recent survey for the government-funded Living Together Campaign, launched to inform cohabiting couples about their lack of rights, found that 61% thought they were in 'common law' marriages, which conferred the same rights as formal wedding vows. The reality is that common law marriage has not existed in England since 1753. (page 8)

■ The myth of common-law marriage springs from a time when there was uncertainty about what constituted a marriage. Church and State marriage ceremonies are relatively recent. (page 9)

■ Statistics show that almost a third of all British households consist of one person, compared with just three per cent in 1950. (page 12)

■ New research from Edinburgh University on the growing phenomenon of solo living has revealed that between the ages of 25 and 44, almost 20 per cent of men live alone, compared to just six per cent of women. (page 12)

■ Supporters of arranged marriages say that divorce rates are lower than among Western society because parents are better able to choose a suitable partner for their children. The counter argument suggests that the pressure of society as a whole and from the two families concerned keeps the marriage together whether it is successful or not. (page 13)

■ More than half of single women were 'very happy with their lives as they are', compared to 46 per cent of men. (page 20)

■ A pre-nuptial agreement is a written contract between parties who are about to get married. The contract terms are intended to bind the parties to a certain future course of action. (page 24)

■ The divorce process is in two stages – a 'Decree Nisi' and a 'Decree Absolute'. A Decree Nisi is an interim stage, granted by the court when the ground for divorce is established. After a period of time, it can be converted into a Decree Absolute, which marks the end of the marriage. (page 27)

■ When relationships break down, the physical and emotional costs can be high. There is a link between relationship breakdown and poor physical and mental health. (page 29)

■ 2003 saw the biggest increase in divorces in two decades. Marriage break-ups rose by 5,755 to 153,490 in 2003 – the third successive annual rise in a single year since 1985. (page 31)

■ Almost half over-50s surveyed by Friends Reunited Dating were looking for 'fun', because they were single, divorced or widowed. The other half said they were looking for marriage. (page 32)

■ The divorce rate rose rapidly between the mid-1960s and mid-1990s reaching 161,000 in 1997 and subsequently levelling out below 150,000 a year. (page 35)

■ Mediation is about a couple directly negotiating their own decisions with the help of a third party. It is an alternative to solicitors negotiating for them or having decisions made for them by the courts. (page 38)

ADDITIONAL RESOURCES

You might like to contact the following organisations for further information. Due to the increasing cost of postage, many organisations cannot respond to enquiries unless they receive a stamped, addressed envelope.

2as1
113A Anerley Road
LONDON SE20 8AJ
Tel: 0700 22 22 700
Email: info@2as1.net
Website: www.2as1.net
2as1 is a new national organisation, primarily representing the Black Community in Britain.
We provide a unique information service which is the ideal 'first port of call' for anyone needing Marriage and Relationship Support.
In times of relationship crisis, the support for the Black Community has traditionally been provided by friends and the extended family network, as opposed to the mainstream counselling service providers.

2-in-2-1
11 Lambourne Close
Sandhurst
Berkshire GU47 8JL
Tel: 01344 779658
Website: www.2-in-2-1.co.uk
Marriage, from planning your wedding, to enriching and enhancing your couple relationship, support through marital problems, and even the challenges of breakdown and divorce is what 2-in-2-1 is all about. Visit the website or write to the above address for more information.

CARE (Christian Action Research and Education)
53 Romney Street
LONDON SW1P 3RF
Tel: 020 7233 0455
Email: info@care.org.uk
Website: www.care.org.uk
CARE is a Christian charity which produces a wide range of publications, all of which present a Christian perspective on moral issues. To find out more, contact them and ask for their Resources Catalogue.

Divorce-Online Limited
Alexander House
19 Fleming Way
SWINDON
Wiltshire SN2 2NG
Tel: 01793 495959
Email: enquiries@divorce-online.co.uk
Website: www.divorce-online.co.uk
Divorce-Online is an independent limited company incorporated in England and Wales. We are not a law firm and do not provide legal advice except through our member law firms and experts who all hold separate legal indemnity insurance.

FamilyOnwards
39 Chartfield Avenue
LONDON SW15 6HP
Email: jillcurtis@familyonwards.com
Website: www.familyonwards.com
Jill Curtis is a senior psychotherapist working in the UK. Over the past three years Jill has developed familyonwards.com, which has over a hundred articles on it and a continually expanding section of reviews of books on family issues.

Futureway Trust
PO Box 6076
WIMBORNE
Dorset BH21 9AL
Tel: 01202 883887
Email: enquiries@futureway.co.uk
Website: www.nmw.org.uk
Marriage Week is run by Futureway Trust, a registered charity.

Joseph Rowntree Foundation
The Homestead
40 Water End
YORK
North Yorkshire YO30 6WP
Tel: 01904 629241
Email: info@jrf.org.uk
Website: www.jrf.org.uk
The Foundation is an independent, non-political body which funds programmes of research and innovative development in the fields of housing, social care and social policy.

The National Youth Agency
Eastgate House
19-23 Humberstone Road
LEICESTER LE5 3GJ
Tel: 0116 242 7350
Email: nya@nya.org.uk
Website: www.nya.org.uk
The National Youth Agency aims to advance youth work to promote young people's personal and social development, and their voice, influence and place in society.

National Family and Parenting Institute (NFPI)
430 Highgate Studios
58-79 Highgate Road
LONDON NW5 1TL
Tel: 020 7424 3460
Email: info@nfpi.org
Website: www.nfpi.org
An independent charity helping to improve family life by campaigning for a more family-friendly society.

One Plus One Marriage and Partnership Research
The Wells
7-15 Rosebery Avenue
LONDON EC1R 4SP
Tel: 020 7841 3660
Email: info@oneplusone.org.uk
Website: www.oneplusone.org.uk
One Plus One is an independent research organisation whose role is to generate knowledge about marriage and relationships – how they work, why they can sometimes run into difficulties and how couples cope when they do.

Resolution
PO Box 302
ORPINGTON
Kent BR6 8QX
Tel: 01689 850227
Email: karen.mackay@resolution.org.uk
Website: www.resolution.org.uk
Aims to promote a constructive and conciliatory rather than an aggressive or angry approach to resolving the problems flowing from marriage breakdown.

INDEX

ACKNOWLEDGEMENTS

The publisher is grateful for permission to reproduce the following material.

While every care has been taken to trace and acknowledge copyright, the publisher tenders its apology for any accidental infringement or where copyright has proved untraceable. The publisher would be pleased to come to a suitable arrangement in any such case with the rightful owner.

Chapter One: Marriage and Cohabitation

The family then and now, © Jill Curtis 2004, *The family today*, © NFPI 2003, *Changing marriage*, © One Plus One, *Breaking uneven*, © Guardian Newspapers Ltd 2005, *Origins of the myth of common-law marriage*, © One Plus One, *Reasons for cohabitation*, © CARE, *Alone and never married*, © Telegraph Group Ltd, London 2004, *Singletons count the cost of being independent*, © cahoot, *Marriage can save you money!*, © 2-in-2-1, *Arranged marriage*, © National Youth Agency, *The truth behind arranged marriages*, © Newsquest Media Group – A Gannett Company (www.asianimage.co.uk), *Significant others*, © Guardian Newspapers Ltd 2005, *Bridget Jones generation is single … and proud of it*, © Michael Blackley 2005, *National Marriage Week*, © Futureway, *With this prenup I thee wed*, © Guardian Newspapers Ltd 2004, *Pre-nuptial agreements*, © DivorceUK, *The dinner party verdict: don't panic about marriage*, © Guardian Newspapers Ltd 2005.

Chapter Two: Separation and Divorce

Divorce, © Resolution, *Legal jargon for divorce*, © TheSite.org, *Why relationship support is important*, © 2as1.net, *Rise in divorces is blamed on the web*, © Associated Newspapers 2004, *For first-time losers in love, life starts again at 50*, © Telegraph Group Ltd, London 2005, *Divorce through the eyes of a child*, © Mills and Reeve, *Together and apart*, © The Joseph Rowntree Foundation 2004, *How to be a good parent after divorce*, © Jill Curtis 2004, *Mediation and you*, © Divorce-Online.

Photographs and illustrations:

Pages 21, 29: Bev Aisbett; pages 3, 8, 33: Don Hatcher; pages 1, 15, 25, 31, 39: Simon Kneebone; pages 19, 27: Angelo Madrid; pages 6, 37: Pumpkin House.

Craig Donnellan
Cambridge
September, 2005